How On Earth Did I Get Here?

Blessings Edwin
Get ready for an amazing
Journey ... and be listening
for your Defining Moment

Happy in HIM

Jani

July 24

HOW ON EARTH DID I GET HERE?

Defining Moments & Divine Appointments

James H. Willis III

ISBN: 9781974178902
ISBN: 1974178900
Library of Congress Control Number: 2017912289
CreateSpace Independent Publishing Platform
North Charleston, South Carolina

DEDICATION

This book is dedicated to my wife, Candi, for loving me unconditionally and making my "here" so happy; to my children and grandchildren, for making my life so entertaining; to Steven, for "tricking" me on that fateful night...I'll be forever thankful; for my Bible-college days—the greatest four-year devotion that anyone could imagine; and to my God, who took me as I was and was willing to change me into who He wanted me to be.

None of this would have been possible without our daughter Pam, who typed my first draft and had to read my handwriting—truly a miracle!

CONTENTS

FOREWORD
by Steve Hopper

I HAVE ASKED the question "How on earth did I get here?" numerous times. I asked the question at the pivotal age of seventeen when a split-second decision landed me in prison for ten years and that painful time when I lost everything due to financial ruin. I asked that question the night I sat in my dark and lonely house, facing a bitter divorce and heartbreaking child-custody battle. I could go on and on and on, but the beauty of life is that I have also asked that question at the birth of each of my four amazing children and when I look at my beautiful wife and the life we have built together. As I live out my dreams and my purpose as an international speaker and author, speaking on stages to thousands of people from all walks of life, I often ask myself—how on earth did I get here?

The famous poet and writer Jorge Luis Borges said the following:

I believe, generally all persons—must think that whatever happens to him or her is a resource. All things have been given to us for a purpose. All that happens to us, including our humiliations, our misfortunes, our embarrassments, all is given to us as raw material, as clay, so that we may shape our art.

But what's it all for?

Over time, I have come to understand that the lives we've been given are a privilege. I learned through the good, the bad, and the ugly that my story was just part of a much bigger story. Having the opportunity to share that story and impact other people's lives is truly a gift, and it's a gift that has eternal significance.

A man who knows that eternal significance well is Jim Willis. Jim is a successful business person with a passion for discipleship. It's been said that there is no one better on a mission field than Jim. I have had the honor and pleasure of not only being friends with Jim, but, on occasion, I have been blessed to receive some of his guidance and mentorship in life. How on earth did I get here? I believe it's partly because of amazing people in my life like Jim Willis.

When Jim first shared his life's journey with me, I was overwhelmed with emotion. His story impacted me in such a way that I decided to feature his testimony in my first book, *From Prison to Purpose.* Jim's story is one of tears and triumph, failure, and success—and of a man overcoming the deepest pain of life to experience the joy and true meaning of life. In the pages of *How on Earth Did I Get Here?* you too will experience the story that is impacting lives all over the world.

Whether you are currently asking how did I get here—on bended knees or asking it full of gratitude for where you are in your life, this is a book that will give hope to the hopeless and encourage the encouraged. You will be so glad you chose to read this book. Join Jim as he opens his heart and shares a journey with you that could answer the very powerful question, how on earth did I get here?

Let the journey begin!
Steve Hopper
Motivational speaker, author, performance coach
www.SteveHopperInternational.com

ENDORSEMENTS

"As a Pastor, the question I most often hear is, "What is my purpose in life?" It's a great question and deserves an answer – not from a Pastor or a Seminary Professor – but from a man who understands what it means to live out his faith and bring glory to God from his home, his office, and his pew. Jim Willis is a man worthy of a read. The tongue in his shoe and the tongue in his mouth go in the same direction. He walks his talk and talks his walk. "How On Earth Did I Get Here?" will help you understand you're here for a reason, and it's a good one. Read it and learn! Enjoy it and share!"

Ken Whitten, Senior Pastor
Idlewild Baptist Church
Lutz, FL

"How on Earth Did I Get Here?" is a question that we all ask but Jim Willis has answered the question with insight and understanding. Knowing Jim had made me familiar with his story, but this book gave me a better understanding of the man and of how God can and does work to save His creation, no matter what the circumstances.

Let me encourage you to get comfortable and pay attention as Jim tells you his story and answers the question, "How on Earth Did I Get Here?".

In God's Grace,
Elbert Nasworthy, Senior Pastor
the church @ Myrtle Lake

"What a great read…Following Jim on this amazing journey is quite a ride! To understand where Jim came from to where he is today is to understand that there is a great God who has a plan for each one of us."

Bob Durham
Area Director
Fellowship of Christian Athletes

"Jim Willis is a disciple who helps others. His life is marked by choices only a follower of Christ would make. He is leading his family and his colleagues down that same path, and his authority and credibility to write "How on Earth Did I Get Here" comes out of his own life as a disciple."

Pastor Rob Taylor
Pastor of Financial Stewardship and Men's Ministry
Idlewild Baptist Church, Lutz, Fl.

ABOUT THE AUTHOR

James H. Willis III (Jim) is an author, an international speaker, and a financial expert who has received multiple awards for his success in the industry. He is the founder and president of The Willis Agency, Inc., a business that focuses on the insurance needs of and financial opportunities for those reaching their retirement years.

He was born and raised in Florida—a true native. Jim grew up without church, without Christ, and without any knowledge of the Bible. His family was so full of conflict that at the age of fifteen, he ended up homeless, alone in the world, and living in a tree. He became involved in the pleasures of the world and was trapped in Satan's devices, learning the survival skills of life while providing for himself.

Jim shares the amazing and sometimes terrifying stories of how he not only survived his homeless years but kept himself in school, graduated, and went on to be successful in business and encourages others who are facing life's insurmountable problems.

At the age of twenty-three, Jim was "tricked" by a friend into going to a religious movie, and he was miraculously saved. For the first time, Jim heard that "somebody" loved him, and he gave his heart to God. Jim knew that God was calling him to preach, and although he was terrified of public speaking, by the time he was twenty-four, he was off to Bible college with the "calling of God" in his heart. At college, Jim learned amazing spiritual truths and graduated with a Bachelor of Science degree in theology—*and* he had conquered his fear of public speaking!

Every one of his stories demonstrates a Defining Moment that may very well have been a Divine Appointment used by God to shape Jim's life. *And now*, thanks to God's love and saving grace, Jim is part of the family of God. He has a heart completely sold out to God, a loving family, and a successful business, and he feels like he is living a dream every day, full of God's peace, joy, and passion in his heart.

INTRODUCTION

**Personal Adventure stories—Experienced
Self-Help concepts—Learned
Spiritual Growth Steps—Impact!**

THE PERSONAL STORIES are amazing adventures I had as a boy, growing up in the woods and waters of Florida. I will also show you the conflicts in my life—the fights within the family, the bullies, the gangs at school, and how I learned to survive. You will see how I went from living in a tree for months at age 15, to where I am today, in successful US suburbia. But it's much more than that. Sadly, nobody looked for me while I lived in that tree. I was tremendously insecure, full of self-doubt, and always in a mood where my anger could violently explode at any time. I was truly homeless and alone, feeling helpless and hopeless. Now, *that's where I started from.*

The *self-help concepts* are the "beginning steps" of what I learned for survival, responsibility, initiative, and goals in life. They continue even to this day. There are also emotional steps, like self-esteem and self-confidence and how to handle anger and conflict. Thus, the real story. How did I find significance in life? How did I get peace? Where did I find love? This book tells my stories. Even as I look back, some of the things that happened to me are just amazing—how did that happen? Or how did that *not* happen? But most amazingly, how did I live through it?

The *Spiritual Growth Steps* show how my life was completely turned around. I went from being unloved, unwanted, and uncared for to the total opposite. I'll tell you how in the book. You see that as we go through life, we all have these "defining moments" where we make choices—sometimes the right one and, well, sometimes the wrong one. Growth of any kind is not by accident, nor is it by osmosis; *it is intentional.* The encounters with God that followed each Defining Moment were huge steps in my life, giving me peace, joy, and love that I never dreamed possible. I got personal growth, fulfillment, and purpose that no one else ever thought probable. The *spiritual transformation* came from simple obedience to God's leadership and His communication in my life.

Out of pure curiosity, people have asked me, "How did you get here from that tree, so unloved and so insecure?" In thinking about the answer to that question, I realized that there were several Defining Moments that were really Divine Appointments. (They are important for everybody.) At those times, I choose to be obedient, and that is when my tremendous growth steps took place.

I share my stories of God's communication with me about each next spiritual step. It's amazing what obedience, faith, and trust will do for your spiritual growth. My stories are unique to me, but my goal is to help you realize that you too have made some or all these steps or that you need to take some of them. Then you will have your own stories of your Defining Moments that may really be Divine Appointments.

This book is individualistic; it is *MY story* — not yours. That's the point and the goal of the book. But you too have a story? These growth steps are for anyone and everyone. What are yours? Which steps have you taken—if any? Why not let the reading of my story be the time you start your story? Listen to yourself—to your story. Listen to what God is telling you and be intentional in your growth.

You can do this! Pay attention to that still, small voice in your life and in your heart, and then act in faith, and obey. Set doubt and worry aside. God's got ya! It is my hope and prayer that my stories will make you laugh and maybe make you cry and that they will give you hope that you too can know how to apply God's leadership in your life and follow Him more intimately.

I was not just surviving but thriving. Give God the glory. Amen!

What will your story be?

1

THE SECOND GLANCE THAT
CHANGED EVERYTHING

S HE WALKED BY me with a first piercing glance, and then she stopped and
gave me that fatal second look. What she said next changed my life immediately and forever.

"She" was my mom, and for the past several years, I had done everything
possible to stay away from home and out of her way. You see, she didn't like
me at all. I didn't know why, at least not at that time. I know; I know; most of
you, when you see your mom, go give her a hug—but not me. I had learned
to run the other way and hide, anything to not be seen. It was never good for
me to be in her presence—bad things always happened.

At that time, she hadn't seen me in weeks. I knew her schedule and stayed
away. I was fifteen and hadn't been home much since the awful divorce when
I was thirteen. Life in our home was so violent—not just words, but actual
hitting and fighting. It was a horrible place for me.

So when she gave me that first glance and walked by, I felt lucky. But
that quickly changed. I was moving fast to get out of her view, but not fast
enough. With that second look, she glared at me and said, "You look just like

your father. I hate him, and so I can't stand to look at you. You need to leave and never come back!" I was fifteen.

I knew she was serious. She was furious at my dad, and, really, so was I, but I needed him badly. I hadn't seen him but once in two years and didn't know where he was. And now, my mother didn't even want to see me. I knew better than to argue with her. It wouldn't have helped, and I didn't like being there anyway. But where would I go? What would I do? How would I take care of myself? Those are all what I call "physical questions."

But the questions that broke my heart, the questions that haunted my soul, and the questions that had no answers were the "relationship questions." Why did she hate me? What was wrong with me? What had I done wrong? Why didn't anybody love me? My dad had disappeared from my life, my older sister hated me, and we physically and verbally fought all the time. And now my mom...I knew she didn't like me, but for her to say she couldn't even look at me and to kick me out of her home forever? It was one of those things that even though I knew it was true, I couldn't believe it was happening. Who does that to their own child? I was fifteen years old and homeless.

Understandably, I had some major insecurities in my life. I had anger and even rage inside of me. I had trust issues with people. I still do, even though I've intentionally worked on it my whole life. I felt completely horrible in every way, even embarrassed. I kept this "family secret" close to my chest. I didn't tell anyone what had happened to me.

I felt completely unloved, unwanted, and uncared for. Oh yes, and we will talk about that some more. At fifteen, a naturally insecure time in anybody's life, I found myself emotionally and physically hopeless, helpless, and now, homeless.

You are probably wondering where I went. What did I take? My mother meant it, and she wanted it to happen right now. You can't even imagine all my thoughts. My brain clogged up. I knew I had to get out of there fast, and I could figure things out later. I was so crushed. I had to get away from even more trouble.

My siblings were home and saw everything, even though it happened so quickly. My little brother was there, but he was too young to know what was going on. There were no good-byes. I had to get out of there as fast as I could. I was through there forever. I grabbed my bike and peddled away, never looking back. I didn't know where I was going, except away!

I was riding hard, not really paying attention to where I was going. After a while, I noticed I was heading toward the woods. I grew up playing in the woods or on the water—my only happy times and places. At that moment, I knew at least one thing; I knew where I was going. I would gather my stuff and go way, way back in the woods and live up in the "Big Tree."

2

WHY LIVE IN A TREE?

I HAVE TO tell you something important. My hero was Tarzan, King of the Jungle. (If you don't know who he is, Google it, and look for Johnny Weissmuller.) Long, long ago, before electronic toys, there were thousands of children playing outside. My friends and I were the "adventurers of the wild."

I was born on a forty-acre ranch in St. Petersburg, Florida, on a corner of my grandfather's property. If we walked down the driveway, turned left, and walked a block, we were in the Gulf of Mexico (actually Boga Ciega Bay). We even had our own beach. We just had to watch out for the bulls. Remember, it was a ranch!

I thrived on the adventures of Tom Sawyer and Huck Finn, and at the age of seven or eight, I "built me a raft" and went poling out into the Gulf of Mexico using an eight-foot pole—twice as tall as I was. Luckily, the tide eventually brought me back to shore. There are so many stories of our adventures on the high seas! OK, they weren't really that "high," but it was in the water, and anything could, did, and does happen.

If I turned right out of the driveway, I was in the greatest woods a boy could imagine exploring, and every day was an unbelievable adventure. As

I look back, yes, it included innumerable life-and-death encounters that, thankfully, we lived to tell about—just like Tarzan and Davey Crockett (you can Google him too). We built forts and tree houses and made swings from the vines in the trees. We could swing from tree to tree—of course, yelling the Tarzan yell—and never touch the ground. We had encounters with every local animal in Florida. And yes, that includes alligators. But the gator stories won't be a part of this book. We're going to take a "spiritual adventure," which can be just as exciting—at least mine is. To understand my story and the title of this book, it is important to understand where *I started from.*

Family wise, my life was a mess; there was nothing but conflicts and fighting. It went from verbal abuse to physical beatings from my parents, and for a reason unknown at the time, my older sister hated me. I didn't think she even liked that I sucked oxygen out of the air. I don't remember a time in my life when I wasn't fighting—yes, with fists—fighting for my life. I also have a little sister. She just wanted everyone to love each other, or, as we say in the South, "Bless her little heart." She was clearly the favorite in the family. The fourth child in the family is a brother, younger by five years. He was too young to be aware of the family conflicts. At an extremely young age, he showed a tremendous connection with animals.

Mom was a poor but beautiful "beach babe." She and my dad, a rich city boy from the country-club scene, got "hooked up," and back then, I'm sure the drama was fit for a soap opera.

Our parents fought all the time. Mom was unhappy, going from the beach scene to staying at home with four kids. One of my few fond memories of her was that whenever one of us got sick or injured, she always took us to the beach. She grew up on the beach, and no matter what was wrong with us, she believed the salt water could fix it. And I think it usually did. I don't remember a time in my life when I couldn't swim. Some of the family say I was swimming before I could walk—just stories, right?

And Dad, he was going for the American dream! His dad, my "papa," was very successful, and so the expectation was set. Dad worked all the time—six days a week, ten- to twelve-hour days—and he progressed quickly through the retail ranks. He was an ambitious, determined man. (Some of that is good, right?)

My home life was in chaos every which way. Luckily, I had lots of friends where I could sleep over a night or two. I saved those nights for when the rage might have a carryover effect. I showed back up when it calmed down.

School helped me keep some regularity to my life, but academically, I didn't do very well. It was always hard for me. Most of it didn't make sense. All through elementary school, I was constantly pulled out of class to get extra reading help. I remember how nice those teachers were, and they tried and cared so much, yet my progress was slow. So, at the age of ten, fifth grade, my parents and teachers decide to keep me back. Even if it was the correct decision, it was devastating to my self-image, which was horrible already. Honestly, I was a hollow, empty shell of a person.

I used humor to cover up a lot of my pain, and people liked it. So as all my peers moved on to the sixth grade, I was held back—for my benefit, of course. Ha! *I did not think so at all.*

So, these new younger fifth graders came in, and of course, I knew several. You know, some kids are nice, and some kids are not. That's just the way it is. And there are always bullies. I've never been a fan of bullies of any kind at any time. I don't like that scenario. I even get frustrated watching it on TV. It's just not right…period!

You would think that I would or could be the bully, being older and stuff. Ha! Nope. No way. I was still the smallest guy in class. That was always the case! I never really liked that, but I dealt with it in several ways. One "skill" that I used frequently was speed. I was fast—really fast. As you know I already had a "chip on my shoulder" most of the time. Well there was this huge kid who was a class bully and thought it was cool to pick on me because I was dumb and got held back. And, of course, it bothered me,

A couple of weeks went by, and he just wouldn't stop. Then one morning, I had gotten into a big fight with my older sister, so I was agitated already, and he started on me as soon as I walked into class. He was standing at the back, and my desk was up front. I put my books down and ran right at him full speed and tackled him to the ground. *Boom!* Chaos everywhere.

Luckily for me, the teacher came in and instantly sent both of us to the principal's office. I'd been there before, but this would be bad. Fighting at school was an automatic three swats (three hits with a paddle on your backside). And though the principal was nice, she was big. She gave the other guy his swats first, and he was crying like a baby and blubbering all over himself. I knew I wouldn't do that…right? Wow, she swatted me good—ouch. I fought back with all that I could. I could take this! I'd been in pain, and I could handle it—so I did. She talked to us for a while — "no fighting, boys"— and sent us back to class.

To my surprise and to our teacher's frustration, the students broke out into a *roar,* clapping for me because someone had finally taken down that big bully. Ha! Despite the backside pain, this was cool.

Those types of stories continued all through my school years. As I went through junior high school, seventh, eighth, and ninth grades (remember, I was a year older than everybody), I was still smaller than all the little seventh graders. It was frustrating, but the girls thought I was cute. Now, that's too funny, isn't it?

In the meantime, my parents didn't get along for all kinds of reasons. In a word, they were dysfunctional, long before it was ever "the word."

Then the most unexpected, uncommon thing happened—they were getting a *divorce*! Understand, in the mid-sixties, this was completely socially unacceptable. Nobody in society circles got divorced. Our world completely collapsed. At thirteen, anything and everything I knew got a lot worse—fast. The violence escalated. I started drinking on the weekends and stayed away as much as possible. A little personal note: I was an insecure little boy. I was a poor learner and student because I couldn't read well. That was personally damaging, so I got a "chip on my shoulder"—quickly. Then add the embarrassment of my sister beating me up. When the kids at school made fun of me, the only way I knew how to fix it was to *beat them up* and say, "See, she could beat you up too." I know it was crazy! But that's my point. How in the world did I get "here" to this secure, happy life that is fulfilling, joyful, healthy, educated, successful, and so on? Yes, I'm living the dream every day! Praise the Lord, God Almighty.

Oh, but wait…I was in the middle of telling you how much *worse* things were getting in my life, wasn't I? OK, back to the bad.

My dad lost his job because Mom was so furious that she kept causing trouble at his workplace. I believe she had a right to be angry, but that meant we had no money—*none*. We lost everything overnight. I didn't see my dad or hear from him for several years.

At that age, obviously, I was out of control. Luckily, I had been working since I was twelve, mowing yards. At thirteen, I started delivering papers on my bike in the afternoon. After that, I worked at a boat dock.

The divorce was bitter and absolutely horrible. I began weekend drinking at the age of thirteen and was gone all weekend—anything not to be at home. Mom's attitude was vengeful, so it was best to stay away. Sometime during ninth grade, when I was fourteen, she decided I had stolen a special ring of hers. I don't know what she thought I would do with it. Hock it? Everyone around us knew everyone else, so that wouldn't have worked. Anyway, I did not steal it, take it, or sell it, but she just *knew* that I had and called the police on me. She called the police on her fourteen-year-old son because she *thought* I had taken something.

Two police officers came to the school to pick up and arrest me, but some friends of mine were in the office (in trouble) and heard them. Luckily for me, they slipped out and came to my class to tell me that the police were looking for me. Wowzers! I decided I'd better get out of there. As the teacher wrote on the blackboard, I rolled out the open window and ran as fast as I could to the woods. The police officers came to my classroom. They found out I had taken off, and the chase began.

I'm just telling you my story here. I don't support these actions, like running from the police, but it happened, and it went down like this. They tried to catch me, but, honestly, nobody could catch me in *my* woods. Nobody! They looked for several hours and never got close. I knew where they were, but they never had a clue where I was or where I was going. Know what they did next? They even got some German shepherd dogs after me, a fourteen-year-old kid, because my mom thought I stole her ring. They tried to catch me for hours in those swamps, lakes, and my favorite tree swings. As kids, we had hooked those vine systems over the limbs and could swing from tree to tree. (I told you Tarzan was my hero!)

I was having a blast. The police were exhausted and left me alone after searching for me for two days. I stayed missing for almost two weeks, until my mom found the ring exactly where she had put it. She told the police that I must have put it back. I knew from my little sister that Mom had found it, but Mom never said anything to me, and I just started back in school again. Not much to do after that, but emotions were building.

You'd think that the year I was thirteen was my worst year ever. I'd like to think so too, but it wasn't. It was when I was fifteen. Two things happened that summer that forever changed my life. The first, as difficult as it was, started off as a positive. Nobody noticed, including me, that I was having a growth spurt.... *finally!* I was *always* the smallest kid in class- always! But unbeknown to all, I was growing. During the summer before ninth grade, I grew seven inches. Yeah!

I made sure I was rarely home except to change clothes or something. But one day I had bad timing. My older sister came home drunk and mad about something. She stared howling at me, and "the fight" began again, for the one thousandth time (one hundred is an underestimate). We both noticed my arms had grown a lot. Every time she came in at me, *pow.* I could jab her with my left. I've got to confess, I was smiling and loving every bit of it! *I* realized she was *never* going to beat me up again, but *she* didn't catch on as quickly. She was as mad as I had ever seen her. This went on for forty to forty-five minutes. Well, let's skip the blow-by-blow, and I'll just end telling you she was so frustrated that she tore up the kitchen because she couldn't tear up me. I left again for several days but with my head held high, knowing it would never happen again. It was over—finally.

It was the summer after ninth grade. I was able to get a lot of work, and I made pretty good money for a kid. Otherwise it was adventures and parties. A couple of weeks went by. I knew the pressure was building, and I kept away from my sister and mother. But I finally had bad timing. My mom came home on a Saturday when I was taking a shower and getting some clothes. I was there so rarely that we were surprised to pass each other. At her first glance, I kept moving, and then there was that fateful second glance. And now we're back to the opening of the book, when I was out of the house, heading somewhere, anywhere, nowhere, and I ended up at "The Tree!"

I had a lot to figure out for a carefree fifteen-year-old kid. Where would I go? What would I do? How would I eat and live? Every decision in life was mine, and it was up to me to accomplish it.

The first problem was where would I live. It was summer, so it was no problem staying at a friend's house for a day or two. That gave me time to set up "my place" way back in the woods. For six months, I lived in that tree. It was a natural place for me to go; it was where I was most comfortable emotionally. This tree was huge, way back almost to nowhere, and safe. I set up place twenty to twenty-five feet from the ground. In some ways, it was spectacular—the breeze, the stars, the quiet, and the amazing variety of animals. It was like camping out all the time.

In other ways, it was very difficult. In the summer in Florida, it rains regularly. There was no lack of adventure as well as no lack of obstacles—like no modern conveniences. Everyday things were certainly a challenge, but I had solutions. There was a nearby lake where I could swim and bathe—with all of Florida's wildlife in that lake with me: fish, turtles, snakes, and alligators. All Florida children grew up swimming in the lakes. Sure, I had to be aware of my surroundings and be "in charge" of them, but I was just like Tarzan, king of the jungle. That's an attitude I still have in the woods.

I also built a fire pit under the tree (it's a *big* tree) for several purposes. I could cook on it, but mostly the fire was built to "slow burn" at night to keep the bugs and mosquitoes away. And lastly, it was for light. The only lights in the woods were the stars. The stars are awesome but hard to study by. It's just like camping. I had to get my act together before it got dark. For me, going to bed included climbing a tree. That meant that when I woke up in the morning, I had to watch my step!

The first month or so was busy. It was probably a good thing since I had a lot on my mind. There was so much to figure out, like how to keep my clothes dry or how to keep some food around without attracting larger animals or having ants and bugs get into my food. It was challenging to say the least. But I was making progress.

It wasn't the Swiss Family Robinson tree house, but it worked for the time. I had different sitting and sleeping places in the tree. One branch was about twenty feet off the ground and had a canopy over it, so I could stay dry. If the rains got bad (we have hurricanes in Florida), I had several friends I could stay with for a night or two. One big branch, way up top was my favorite place on earth. There was a breeze, no bugs, and the stars—wow! It was absolutely beautiful.

I was also alone. Some of that was good, and some was, well…alone. All the thoughts inside of me came to the surface of my mind. It was usually stuff like nobody loves you, you are a nobody, you will never amount to anything, or look what your other friends have! Thankfully I had a lot of friends, but all of them were living the great American family life. Mine was a nightmare. I didn't want to talk to anybody about all this—I was way too embarrassed. I learned to talk to the stars at night, but my conversations turned into me standing at the top of that tree, hollering every profane word I knew at the top of my lungs.

There seemed to be plenty of cussing and yelling in the middle of the nights, blaming my parents and family for everything. I was all by myself, and I was letting them have it. Were my thoughts true? Was I a nobody, worthless, no good, nothing? Perhaps, but something else happened after those midnight cries for help as I sat at the top of the tree. There was a quiet voice, a soft voice or thought. It was me saying, "I want to be a somebody. I'm not a nobody; I can be a somebody. I'm not going to be a nobody!" I have to tell you, I liked those words, yet I had no reason to believe them. But I wanted to believe them. I wanted to be a somebody.

This went on for weeks. I was into the routine of blaming everybody and I was getting pretty good at it to tell you the truth. Then on one crystal clear, starry, beautiful night, a new thought blasted into my head. "Jim, you are still in the tree. You can blame them all you want, but you are still in the tree. If you want to get out of this tree and get out of your circumstances, then *you* are going to have to do something about it. Jim, it's up to you—*nobody else.*"

I fell back onto the tree. Don't worry. By this time, I was as agile as the monkeys and cheetahs, and I just fell into the limbs as if they had caught me. *It's up to me to get out of this tree.* I could go through life blaming other people for my problems, or I could overcome them myself. I wanted to believe I could, but I really had nothing to show for it. Everybody thought I was a nobody, and none of the people who were supposed to love me wanted me around. That put me pretty far down in terms of value as a human being. I mean, I was living in a tree, people. I was helpless, hopeless, and homeless. But I decided *that* has *all* got to change.

MY LIFE NEEDED TO TAKE FOUR LARGER-THAN-LIFE STEPS

First, I had to get honest with myself. I was *discouraged*! This was an understatement! I could fake it (and in public I did), but it didn't change anything. I realized that I just needed to admit to myself (not necessarily to the whole world) that, yes, I was bitter, that I had a lot of resentment inside of me, and that I was downright mad! I also figured out it didn't matter what anyone else did wrong, so I could pass the buck or pass the blame to someone else. I was still in that tree, and only I could take the responsibility to get me out of there and into a building, apartment, home…anything! Important note here: I didn't believe for one second that someone else should get me out of that trouble. I always felt that it was up to me, not other people to fix my problems. I've heard it said, "The best helping hand you can have is at the end of your arm." I needed to stop the self-pity and become self-reliant and depend on myself—not on others.

Second, I realized I needed to be *determined.* What I needed to do was get rid of all my excuses (and boy, did I have plenty of them) and show people and myself that I was a somebody and not a nobody. I also realized that I wanted and needed to work hard—harder than most to prove my worth and growth. And I was determined to have some peace and calm in my life—no more arguing and fist fighting. I needed to calm down and find out how to take it easy in this horrible world I was in.

Third, I realized I needed to be *disciplined* and nonconforming. I couldn't just do what everyone else was doing because my circumstances were so different. I had to figure out how to change my values and find different friends with those same values and start living differently. I knew I needed to grow up, and fast, but how? I would find some older people I trusted, ask questions, and get advice. I also decided that if I have troubles, so do others, and I should start trying to help other people, not just myself. By the way, helping others was both fun and fulfilling and made me think better of myself, which was very important.

Fourth, I realized I needed to be a *dreamer*. As unrealistic as that seemed, it was the hope that kept me alive. I had a good imagination—remember, I was living like Tarzan, king of the jungle. Ha-ha! But now my personal thoughts couldn't be just for fun; I had to stop all the negative stuff and choose to be positive. I would focus on positive thoughts that were reinforced with positive action, like helping others. I would use positive self-talk to pump myself up, and I still do that today. I kept thoughts like "You can do this," "Just keep it up; you'll get out of this," or "You're awesome, Jim; you can do it!" I learned quickly to keep these thoughts to myself and be humble around others. I wanted to be somebody and not a nobody, which was what everyone was saying, and it hurt—bad. But I refused to believe that I was a nobody. I had this thought inside my head, especially at night in the tree: "I want to be a somebody! I will be a somebody." It was haunting back then, but here's what I figured out. Not a single person wants to be a nobody! Anybody can be a somebody, and everybody has a choice: you can be a nobody or a somebody. I knew I might be a nobody now, but I was willing to do whatever it took to be a somebody. It was a driving force in my life; it was my dream—as unrealistic as it might have seemed at the time.

So, don't feel like you are a nobody. Anybody can be a somebody. Keep reading! I'll explain more later in the book. I know it to be true.

3

GETTING OUT OF THE
TREE - SURVIVAL SKILLS

THE STORY CONTINUES with me in tenth grade, living in a tree and keeping myself in school. Yes, I kept myself in school. I even registered myself. I found myself in a public-speaking class, a course everybody had to take back then. I'd never really done that before. The first assignment was a three-minute speech about what you did that summer. Oh, ouch! I didn't think I should tell everybody about the victory fight with my sister or how my mom couldn't stand to look at me and kicked me out of the house. And I really didn't want to tell everybody how I felt and what was going on in my life. I was stumped, and of course, there was no one to talk to about it. I finally came up with an animal adventure story. I had those all the time, and people seemed to be amazed by them.

The day came, and the teacher called my name. "Mr. Willis, your turn to speak." By this time in my life, I wasn't really afraid of anything. I had already experienced so many natural and unnatural situations, and I was game for anything. Remember, I've confessed I have an adventurous spirit.

I got up in front of the class, ready to tell my story. I knew everybody. I had grown up with most of them. I was shocked by what happened. My hand clasped that aluminum podium, and I froze. I couldn't look up, my tongue got thick, my knees were getting weak, I started to sweat, and my heart pounded so hard I thought people could hear it. I stood there for what felt like at least five minutes (thirty seconds really). I never said a thing, not one word, and I sat back down, in front of course. I was *totally embarrassed.* Oddly, I don't remember anybody saying or doing anything to make fun of me. As nice as that was, *I knew I would never speak in public again.* But I had to take this class, and I had to figure out a way to pass. I'm not a failure—right?

I'll never forget Mr. Scott, the teacher. I sat quietly through the class, listening to all the speakers. Some were pretty good. I waited to the end to say anything. As the bell rang, I stood up, and so did he. We called out each other's names. I said that I needed to find out a way to get a C in the class without ever speaking, and he, without hesitation, said to come to wrestling practice today at four.

You see, he was the wrestling coach. When I got to the practice, the guys were already warming up, and he and I made a deal. If I would be the wrestling manager all season, he would give me a C. I asked what a manager did. His first comment was, "Whatever I say." I agreed to all his requests. I was in charge of all the clean and dirty towels, the sweaty mats, water, and so on.

He eventually got me sparring with some of the other guys—just practicing with them. Even with my growth spurt, my official weight was 128. He quickly saw that I was scrappy and fast, and he kept moving me around to different weight classes, I think mostly to help them with their speed. I did fine until they caught me. Ouch! I enjoyed it though. I got rid of a lot of pent-up frustration.

Then there were the matches. Wowzers! Intense and cool. Then, out of the blue, a guy didn't make the weight limit, so Mr. Scott called me over and said, "Hey, Jimmy, we don't have anybody, so why don't you give it a try? Go ahead. We've got nothing to lose."

I was somewhere between being a complete nervous wreck and excited to be allowed to do "controlled fighting." I was all game. Even though I didn't know many moves or the rules very well, I figured it was only three one-minute time frames. Wow, was I surprised and exhausted, but I lasted all three rounds. I lost in points, but I didn't get pinned. I thought that was OK.

Mr. Scott seemed pleased, and I liked that. Hey, someone liked what I did, and I hadn't really experienced much of that lately. Over the season, he threw me out on the mat at every different weight class. I held my own. I even won a few. It was fun, but it was the responsibility that I enjoyed most. And yes, I got a C in public speaking. Job complete!

I never knew if Mr. Scott knew about what had happened to me as far as my homelessness, living in a tree, family divorce, and stuff. But unknowingly or not, he had a positive impact on my life during a turbulent time. You can see that I learned early how to wheel and deal and get through life. More of that coming.

Transportation was always a challenge. I had a newer, faster ten-speed. They had just come out. It was cool and fast, and I could get places in no time, day or night. The problem was that I was carrying stuff like school supplies, clothes, and groceries, and it just wasn't practical. It was hard to get it back into the woods—I mostly carried it. So, I exchanged it for a more practical bike. It had high handle-bars, the banana seat, and two saddlebags on the back for packing. I adapted it to be mostly rainproof too. It wasn't as fast, but it was much more useful.

Finally, I was getting close to turning sixteen and would be able to drive, but I had to take the driving test. I needed to practice, and I needed a car. I made a surprise visit to the house to see if Mom would let me use her yellow Volkswagen Beetle. It was cool and easy to drive. I'm not sure she realized I had been gone. We argued a little, and then she let me take it for a test drive—with her. Oh boy, *was that a mistake!*

She hollered at me to do this and that and look here and there. It was awful. I ended up a nervous wreck and just stopped the car in the middle of a neighborhood. We continued arguing, but I somewhat convinced her that I had been practicing with some friends' cars and was doing fine. I just needed her car for the test. Reluctantly, she finally agreed.

We arranged to meet on my birthday, June 13 to go to the sheriff's office. I wasn't sure she'd go through with it, but she showed up with that wonderful frown she can have and took me. I was so excited, and everything went smoothly at the sheriff's office. The driving test was a breeze, and driver's license in hand, we left. *Yes!* Now I needed a car.

I had been shopping with great expectations, and I had found one close by. Now I had to convince Mom to go with me to help buy a car. She was shocked and determined *not* to help. I explained to her that I didn't need any money; I had my own. I had already looked at the car, but they wanted a parent there since I was under twenty-one. Also, I didn't know how to do the paperwork on the title, and I didn't trust people very much for obvious reasons. So Mom, with that famous frown on her face, went with me to hopefully purchase a car.

An hour later, I pulled out $400 to buy a 1962 white Impala with a red interior. I shocked everyone with the cash. We did the paperwork, and the car and title were mine. The salesperson and my mom were still standing in the yard talking as I drove off. This was a huge life change for me—*a car.*

It was a tremendous step of success for me, great transportation to everywhere. And I went everywhere too—school, work, St. Pete beach, dates, and on and on. It was an easy place to sleep if it was raining. By the way, do you have any idea how much it rains in Florida? It rains only for a short time but frequently. The car itself was a big game changer.

In high school, I was one of the first to drive because of my age. So that was neat. I certainly didn't have a new car like several of my friends, but, hey, it was mine, and I took great care of it.

We would all get together for a day trip to go tubing at Blue Run, Rainbow Springs, or Crystal River. There were six, eight, or ten cars flying up the road early on a Saturday morning going tubing. Great old-fashioned fun. We'd have a great day, and then caravan through the central Florida orange groves to Hillsboro State Park where there was a pool. We hung out till almost dark, and then we all headed back home. Other times, a big group would go to Daytona or Cocoa Beach for a weekend for some awesome surfing and just hanging out. We mostly slept right on the beach; back in those days, it was legal. You can still drive on parts of Daytona Beach today.

I had that Impala for several years, and it always got me where I needed to go (thanks to some mechanical friends). I had nobody telling me what to do and nobody harassing me. I thought life was finally taking a positive turn.

There was an apartment/hotel not far from the restaurant where I worked, and I approached them to see if I could rent a place. The owner just laughed at me. "Hey, kid, where's your parents?"

I said, "They're gone, and I really need a place to stay."

"You're not old enough, kid. You have to be twenty-one to sign the rental agreement."

I was sixteen and a very young sixteen in looks. I said, "I'm homeless, living in the woods up in a tree. I really need a place to live."

He said, "I don't know, kid. I'd get in a lot of trouble."

I said, "Look, I really need some help. I have the money. I work right down the road. I can pay you every Friday at four o'clock." I had about $200. Weekly rent was $50, and I said, "See? I can pay you."

By now, he was trying to figure out what to do. Then he blurted out, "OK, kid, you can have the place in the far back, upstairs, but don't have any parties. Got it?"

Wowzers. Yes, sir! I slapped that fifty bucks on the counter. Luckily, the apartment was partly furnished, dry, and air-conditioned. Nice.

It worked out for a couple of months, but some of the other residents started noticing there weren't any parents and made some comments to him. I had kept a low profile, especially going to school, wrestling, and work until eleven, five nights a week or more. But still, he caught me one morning heading to school. "Hey, kid, I'm gonna get in trouble. You're gonna have to leave."

I asked if I could stay till Friday.

"Sure but keep it quiet."

We had become somewhat friendly. I know he was extremely curious about my situation, but I always kept that close to my chest. But, hey, I've got to figure out what to do next—*fast*. In those few months I was in the apartment, when I went back to the tree—wow—it was going to need some work. The weather in Florida is damaging—either rain or simply heat through the summer. And, oh yeah, the bugs—we have lots of bugs. I've had them crawl on me, and I've played with them. Most just pass by. But there are some—yeah, I just didn't like mosquitoes.

An upper classman named Jim Lamping had been friendly with me. His parents were divorced too. You must realize that people just didn't get divorced back then. Jim and I didn't run in the same social circles, but we had

JAMES H. WILLIS III

several things in common, particularly cars. He was quite mechanical and loved all those new muscle cars and had several. *Wowzers.* They were powerful and crazy fast. We spent time just learning precision shifting—for drag racing, of course. Or we'd practice where the four corners of our cars were. In other words, we practiced pulling up to within three to six inches of objects—it was fascinating to really know my car.

Jim's sister had gone off to college, and they had an extra room. He suggested I move in and pay his mom the fifty dollars weekly. What a life! I was out of that tree. I was high and dry, with electricity and running water. The tree was entertaining but not completely a home. It was great to get back into a house.

It was also nice that *finally* someone cared about my, let's just say, situation or predicament—as in homeless. His mother's name was Syble. She was busy but always friendly and nice. I was able to stay there for about a year and a half.

During this time, our country was having major racial issues between the blacks and whites. It was awful. It was violent. It was intense. It was scary. And it came to our high school. Bussing, segregation, and riots. I had never experienced anything like it. I certainly didn't understand it. But nevertheless, I was right smack dab in the middle of it. We all were. None of us wanted to be there, but the emotions and drama were high. It was *tense,* to say the least.

Now before I go further, I have some personal background that I feel is important to share. My grandparents had a maid, and, yes, she was black. She was wonderful, a sweetie in every way, and very huggable. I had been to her house several times. I had never been taught any difference or prejudice.

My grandfather was the manager of a huge store, and he had employees of many colors and many cultures. I hung out, listening to their stories and, of course, their songs.

As a young teen, I had a job delivering the afternoon *Evening Independent* on my bike. Every afternoon, I went to the paper station and wrapped the papers up in rubber bands if it wasn't raining or in plastic if it was. I rode my bike all over the neighborhood and made many acquaintances. It was fun.

I found early in my life that I was fascinated with people of all kinds, all colors, and all class of economy. I had biker friends, hippie friends, jocks, rich, and normal friends.

I have loved variety all my life. If you know my story today, you know I love going on short-term international mission trips. I've been to Europe, Asia, Africa, Central America, South America, and North America dozens of times, working with all cultures.

I love people—all kinds of people. I don't like "mean" people, though. They're just mean. I stay away.

But getting back to the racial riots. I want to share part of the story that perhaps most of you have never heard before. Because for me—yes, I was young—and it was complicated. I had no idea what was going on in our country. I had my own problems and no TV. I also didn't share a lot of the feelings or beliefs that evidently many others did. Yet there I was, and I had friends…black and white. I had friends on both sides!

It's the same today. I'm friends with everyone if I can. Yet I still remember those god-forsaken days when there were hundreds of white guys on one side of the road and hundreds of black guys on the other side, and twenty-five to thirty cop cars in the median to keep us apart, because we all had something in our hands to fight with. It went on for months. And that was actually the safest time of the day. Moving from class to class was really dangerous, and everything could erupt in a second—and it frequently did. It got to where we would literally fight for your lives. I was nowhere near the biggest, but perhaps one of the fastest.

To protect our black and white friends, we had to come up with something to diffuse the situation when we faced off, gang versus gang, particularly in the much smaller yet unequal settings where it might be two against five. We couldn't be traitors, right? So, we'd say to each other or to our friends, "Hey, guys, you don't want to mess with that guy. I heard he gets crazy and bites when he fights." Nobody ever liked to get bitten—rabies, you know. So we hollered at each other and went our separate ways. I don't know how many times my friends saved me from a fight and I did the same for them. They were hard, hard days for our school, our city, and our country.

Prejudice of any kind is a horrible thing. Whether it is about skin color or economic levels or language, it's awful. The hate does not accomplish anything positive. Stop it. Get over it. Don't let anyone fill your soul with that kind of hate, because your soul will just slowly rot from the inside out. Begin caring for others instead. *Be nice.* Try it; you'll like it.

The following years calmed down quickly with only a few incidents. Progress was happening, and we could be friends again. I had a lot of other things I wanted to be doing in high school besides fighting. There were girls, parties, hangouts, and so on. I also worked full time all through high school. I was a busy guy. I still am!

Those stories of the "good ole" high-school days go on and on, and so much of it was just a repeat each weekend.

Remember that during these years, I was going it mostly alone. I heard about "how cool" my mom was from friends who went to the bank where she worked. It was sad because that was *not* the case for me. I asked myself all the time why she was so nice to everyone else and so mean and hateful to me. I learned quickly to smile and say nothing about our relationship. My dad was gone, who knew where, and I hadn't heard from him for several years…nothing. Nada. By now my older sister was out of school so I had no contact with her—thankfully. Yet I do have this "little sis." She was a grade behind me. She was always the sweet one in the family. In school, she was popular (very cute), which led to a lot of boys in her life. She also had lots of girlfriends, and that was good for me. I still have some of those friends in my life...because of her.

My days and evenings became intense. I wasn't able to do the schoolwork. I just didn't know how to study, nor was I a good reader *at all*. What was wrong with me that I couldn't figure out this reading stuff? It was sad, frustrating, and very defeating. I still faced a lot of daily pressure, anger, frustrations, bad decisions, and the wrong people. My whole life was becoming more and more violent and almost completely out of control.

The summer before my senior year, my dad somehow found me. There were no cell phones or Internet back then, and I was moving fast in life. He wanted to get back in my life. I wasn't sure about that. He contacted me several times. My dad never was much with words—actions, yes. Despite his tremendous sales ability, when it came to his kids, he just didn't know how to talk to us. So there was always a lot of "reading between the lines" and there weren't too many lines to go by.

Several things were coming together. My friend Jim had graduated and gone to the air force. He already had a pilot's license. He clearly loved it, so my place to stay was questionable. I had several, let's just say, "bad relationships" that were only getting worse. I decided to leave South St. Pete and all my friends. I headed to North St. Pete and stayed with my dad and his new wife.

It was interesting, with a new school, new friends, and a new job. I kept working a lot, and I was living with my dad again. Remember, the first thirteen years with him weren't that great. At least now I didn't have my mom or older sister telling stories or falsehoods about me. At least we had a chance, but it was so-so at best.

For my senior year in school, I took it as easy as I could. It was an "open school," so I was only at school when I had classes. I had very few classes because I got into the Diversified Career Technology (DCT) program. That means I got several school credit hours for working. Yes! Less schoolwork and more work making more money. Even at that young age, I had already learned that money helped me do and have things, and I liked that.

Nobody was giving me anything, so I quickly learned that I had to go out and get it. I got a couple of part-time jobs that senior year. I made friends quickly in the new school, which was great. But back at Dad and Sandi's place, it was *awkward* because it was "Sandi's place." I just didn't fit. She did work hard to fit me in, and I've always appreciated that. She was only ten years older than I was, and I was a teenage boy who was different than anyone she had come across.

I wasn't there often, really, hardly at all. I mostly slept there. I left for school at seven thirty in the morning, had a few classes, hung out with friends, and then went off to my first job (for credit for school) from one to five at a lighting company, and then to a toy-and-game warehouse. I liked that job, working in the evenings. If I wasn't working, I was out with friends. I didn't get home till ten thirty or eleven, and Dad and Sandi were asleep. Once in a while, I would be home for dinner, and we'd try to talk, usually with Sandi carrying the conversations. It wasn't bad or good; it just was.

Looking back on that time, I feel it was an opportunity lost for both Dad and me. Neither he nor I went back to the past to work out our feelings and our relationship going forward. It left me even more confused, questioning if he knew what had happened to me or cared. Nevertheless, I came to understand that he does care but really doesn't know how to communicate it with words. That was frustrating and hard to understand. But I knew he cared for me, and I left it at that.

Graduation was coming. No more school! You know that old classic song, "School's out for summer / School's out forever!" Wow, that was my theme song! (It was new back then. You can laugh at me if you want to, but it was a great time for great music that we still listen to today.) I was really excited about graduation. A couple of weeks earlier, I'd gone into the school office to confirm that I was graduating—it was that close, but I felt I had made it, and I did. I had the grades *barely*—all on my own. As messed up as I was, I was going to graduate high school…alive! Back in those days, I qualified as one of those kids who really didn't do that well, but it was better to pass them than to keep them in school. I was "rolled out" of the education system just to get me out of it.

About three days before graduation at the large city auditorium, I started hitting *all the parties*. I was eighteen, to be nineteen in a week, and at the time, eighteen was "legal." So, me coming to the parties helped everybody because I could get the beer. I was a busy happy guy. I had taken a couple of days off to celebrate, so it was nonstop fun and partying.

I was such an uncontrolled mess that I almost missed my own graduation. When we got there, all the talking was over, and they were handing out the diplomas. Kids were already walking up on the stage. Luckily, I was a *W* for Willis, and I had made the practice at school, so I knew who I was sitting beside. I barely made it there physically and mentally. In less than ten minutes, they called my name, and I got my diploma. I was done. I did it. Nobody believed I could, and really, not too many cared, but I did it.

Through all the fighting at home and at school, through all the crazy living conditions—in a tree for months, as an illegal resident in an apartment complex, in an older friend's house, and even a year back with my dad—I did it. At the time, I was a poor learner and probably a worse student because of all the emotional baggage I carried around, knowingly and unknowingly. I learned to travel light, but my heart was both heavy and empty. I filled that *void* continually with this huge social party lifestyle, and this cost me big time on graduation day.

I had been partying with the North St. Pete kids, but on graduation day, I hooked up with a big group of lifelong South St. Pete friends. They were celebrating and begged me to join them and catch up. Good times for all.

As I left the party, I was thrilled. I was elated, overcome with achievement, and *plastered*. I was *not* paying attention, and I ran a red light. The consequences were explosive.

4

ADULTHOOD - WOWZERS! CAN I DO IT?

A N ELDERLY COUPLE was coming through the intersection, and we nailed each other. The sound was like a *bomb* going off. We hit so hard that my precious Volkswagen van went flying forward, and the front windshield exploded in my face. I was just inches from the road's asphalt, and the van flopped over on its side. I wasn't dead, but I wished I was. I was just lying there. I wasn't even hurt, but I was thinking, "I've even ruined my high-school graduation."

I was so sad and so depressed. While living at Dad's, I was making good money, and I didn't have to pay rent. So I had bought this Volkswagen van and fixed it up nicely. I upgraded the sound system and put red shag carpet on three-inch foam, cork ceiling, and red-patterned curtains—great comfort and sounds. I often headed to the beach late at night and lay back, listened to the waves, and went to sleep. It was my getting peace time, and I loved it. (Hey I still do!) But now my Volkswagen was gone. It was ruined.

I know the van was totaled, and it was my fault. I had really blown it this time. There were many other times in my life when I easily blamed my problems on others, but not this time. This was all my fault! My soul was so heavy;

it ached with helpless pain. I had felt it several times in the past, but this time it was supposed to be my day of celebration, and it came to a screeching halt (pun intended).

After a few seconds of self-pity, I realized that I had hit an elderly couple. As I scrambled to get out of my van to check on them, they were both getting out of their car to check on me. What a relief that was. I sure didn't want to hurt someone else.

I can't tell you how crushed I was. All my plans for a new life past high school were thrown into a severe tailspin to say the least. I did get another car in a few days; I had some money and insurance, but I was so embarrassed. My dad knew about it, my North St. Pete friends knew about it, and my South St. Pete friends knew about it. It was like this huge, self-inflicted open wound that everyone could see. I was so embarrassed and so ashamed, and yep, I said it, "I was a failure, even on graduation day!"

I was such a mess. At eighteen, I felt like I had lost everything again. I just disappeared for several days. I went to "the tree" and stayed there for a couple of days, running in the woods by day and howling at the moon and stars, "What's wrong with me? Why did this have to happen?" and on and on.

You may have some of these pains and awful feelings, but let me tell you, you can overcome this. You *are* somebody. You can make a difference in this life. You can find happiness, fulfillment, and purpose. You can have peace, forgiveness, and love. You can have financial success if you want it. We are getting closer to how I found my way, but there are a few more stories to share.

After the crash, I had to come back into life again whether I liked it or not. My two jobs were looking for me. Dad and Sandi were wondering where I was, and I had been dating a girl I had met in North St. Pete for most of the senior year, Laura, and she was concerned for me.

So at least this time when I was in "the tree," people cared for me. I guess you could call that a step up, but I sure didn't feel like it at all.

So step by step, I started putting my life back together. First, I caught back up with everyone, and they seemed to really care for me. It was nice, but what a mess. It was hard living inside someone, myself, who was such a failure. Workwise, I was working two jobs, one at a lighting store for school credit, and the other at a toy-and-game warehouse that had future opportunities. I talked to them to get more hours, and they were glad, and so was I. I dropped the lighting store, which would have ended after school anyway—and was back to making good money again. I liked the job at the warehouse and grew into it well. I got several raises, seniority, and responsibility.

My living quarters had to change. I had no need or desire to stay at Dad and Sandi's place, so I start looking for an apartment. In the meantime, Laura was obviously making life-changing plans, and we decided to move in with each other. She had a good job as well, so money wasn't a problem, and we really liked each other. We were a cute little couple of "love birds." I still remember her as being sweet and nice. I had had several nice girlfriends over the years. It was a continual bright spot in my life, but somehow, I would get frustrated and break up the relationship. Laura was much more "with it" in life than I was. But most everybody was.

We moved in together. It was very exciting and nerve-racking, but for the first time in my life, I was living with someone who liked (loved) me. There were so many pieces of life's puzzles to put together, like our work schedules and fixing up the apartment. (I had no ideas there.) There were our meals, our personal space, and our relaxation and recreation. It was a lot for me to take on emotionally, yet she was having fun, and we were doing well for several months.

Then I started to withdraw within myself. It was all too much at one time. I think she could and did handle it well, but I became a wreck. Even now as I look back at that time, I have so many regrets.

You see, here is an important point: if you aren't happy with yourself, you won't be happy with someone else. In other words, if you aren't comfortable in your own skin, you won't be happy with someone else's skin. It became frustrating for us both for it not to work out, but I wasn't getting around the corner and communicating well, so we split up. Communication is still the key in relationships.

It was sad. She went back home. I stayed there until the lease was up.

Then I moved into a great singles apartment complex. I thought that this would fix everything. It sure kept me distracted from the pains of life inside my soul. The job was going great and was stable with room to grow. The new place had lots of friendly people, if you know what I mean. There were parties almost nightly as well as group activities like going to the beach or whatever we thought to do. My life was good…really good! I worked hard and loved it, and I played harder and loved it. There's no reason to embarrass myself with all the stupid stuff we did and did repeatedly. The point is that I did survive it with great fun, but it was insane.

I was running hard with work and play. Youth can do anything. But was I running *from* something? From what? I made sure I didn't slow down enough to find out. Lots of people, lots of parties, and lots of drinking. As I look back on this time in my life (as I look back on several other times in my life), I know I'm lucky to still be alive. I continually drank and drove. *Don't do that, people—it's stupid!* During this time, I felt like Superman, but while driving drunk, I was in five car accidents. That's right, five of them. Luckily only two were with someone else. I am so thankful that I didn't hurt anyone, and as crazy as some of these accidents were, I never got hurt either. It cost me a lot of money to get another car, and, oh my, my car insurance was more than my car payment. It was awful.

You would think that after the high-school graduation incident, I would never do that again, but I was an irresponsible, functioning, drunken idiot.

But hey, I was a nice guy and lots of fun to be around at parties. I worked hard and paid my bills. I wondered what everyone's problem was. The point is that it wasn't their problem. It was mine. And I still didn't see it or admit it, because life was good. I was just stupid!

In the meantime, Dad caught up with me again. He and Sandi had opened a men's clothing store, and he wanted me to come work with him. Me inside, dressed up, and working with "them"? Oh gosh, no, but thanks anyway! He kept trying to get me to come aboard because he needed help. They expanded to a men's and women's clothing store and called it Pacer's Men's and Women's Clothing Store. "Great for you, but I'm good where I'm at, Dad," I told him.

Finally, he caught me again. I was still saying no when he threw out the question I wasn't ready for because, well, nobody has ever asked me, "How much do you make weekly, Jim?"

I answered, "You can't afford me, Dad."

"How much, son?"

I told him it was $400.00 a week. (That was a lot back then.)

He said, "OK. I'll pay you five hundred dollars a week." *Wowzers.* That would cover an awful lot of twenty-five- and fifty-cent raises. I have no problem telling you that I was bought out by my dad. And, who knew. Maybe we could do a better job rebuilding our relationship through work.

By the way, that was *a lot* of money back in 1973. That weekly salary was more than my monthly rent and then some. The $400 and $500 was only more fuel for the party.

It was quite a learning experience at the store. I bought quite a few clothes at a 50 percent discount. I was styling. Remember way back when leisure suits were made of 100 percent polyester and bell-bottom pants were twenty inches wide at the bottom? We had those and a ton of long-sleeved silk shirts along with patent-leather boots and shoes in nine colors. It was disco time. Hysterical. We sold traditional clothing as well.

The store itself was a middle-upper-class store on Central Avenue and Twentieth Street in St. Pete. The "downtowns" were still popular, but the malls were opening and taking all the traffic. People didn't just walk into our store, they made it a point to come by, and we made sure they had a good experience. Dad had a well-stocked bar in the back. We served liquor, wine, and beer for their shopping pleasure. Isn't that crazy? But people loved it and told their friends. Plus, we had the "new" rock and roll music playing in the background.

Dad figured out a characteristic about me that he used to increase our business. "Jim, you have a way with the seniors. When they come in, be sure to take all of them, and I'll take the business professionals." I think he was tired of the seniors, but I loved them. I had a great clientele of seniors coming to see me. Dad was impressed. He even got more clothes in for me to sell: "portly" coats and suits to fit our happily fed retirees. But when we weren't selling, there was *a lot* of standing around. It was awful. I went stir-crazy, looking out the large glass windows and watching the world go by.

When we were in the store, my dad was in his element. He was almost a completely different man. As a salesman...*wow*. I would watch him masterfully move people along to what they wanted and eloquently and effortlessly suggest this mix and match. I did all I could to copy his process. He saw and said he was...wait for it..."proud of me." How about that? It was the first time.

We ended each day having a drink or two together and reviewing the day and counting the money. Retail business has its ups and downs. Here's a smart business idea he instilled in me: don't spend all you get. Set some aside for the slow days.

On Fridays and Saturdays, both the men's and women's departments were an all-day party. Many of the local car-lot guys came in to buy clothes and hang out, and they brought their lady friends. It was a completely crazy party atmosphere. We could make some good money on those days.

Add to that the exciting singles-only complex I lived in, and my life was party hardy, baby. *Wowzers.* So things went smoothly for about two years.

And then came that fateful last Tuesday of February in 1975. Steven, an old high-school friend of mine who I hadn't seen in years, stopped by and set in progress the biggest change I'd ever had in my life.

5

TRICKED BY A FRIEND!

ALL THESE STORIES have shown me going further and further down into the pleasures and cares of this world. But, more importantly, they show where "there" was before I got "here." The second half of the book will show me growing into a new life that had previously been perhaps just a dream. I'll show you the story, the moment, the appointment, and the time in my life, when I knew God was talking to me. There are Defining Moments in our lives that are actually Divine Appointments. I'm sharing those with you.

First, let's recap the highlights. I am one of four children, born into a typical, ambitious middle-class family. Our lives were full of conflict, with verbal abuse and physical fighting all the time. When I was thirteen, my parents went through a bitter divorce. My dad disappeared for several years, and I began weekend drinking. When I was fifteen, two events took place. My older sister couldn't beat me up anymore because I finally grew enough to defend myself. The second event was that my mom came home one day, stopped in her tracks, and said, "You look just like your father. I can't stand to look at him, and I want you to leave and never come back." So at fifteen, I was homeless, helpless, and hopeless.

Today my family has a phrase that we say jokingly, about being unloved, unwanted, uncared for, but back in those days, they were all completely true. Living in a tree in the woods, I had plenty of time to vent my frustrations. By the time I was sixteen, I had all the world's pleasures at my fingertips. I finished high-school living in a singles-only apartment complex and all the activity that goes with that. Then, my father showed up after not seeing me for several years and wanted to build a relationship. I thought we'd try. I started working at his clothing store in downtown St. Petersburg called Pacers Men's and Women's Wear.

Back to my story. When I was twenty-two, an old high-school friend of mine, Stephen, stopped by the store. Stephen and I had gone through everything together back in the day. When he showed up, he looked just like what, at that time, we called a "Jesus freak." If you saw Jesus in a magazine back in the seventies, he probably had long, dirty-blond hair; a ridiculously big grin; a tie-dyed T-shirt; bell-bottomed jeans; and flip-flops.

To tell you the truth, it made me laugh, and the first thing I said to him was, "What are you, a Jesus freak?"

He said, "Yeah, man. I found God."

I had heard something like that before, but none of that meant anything to me. I had never been to church or read a Bible. I didn't even know many Christians and stayed away from them. But Stephen and I had been best friends at one time, so I continued to catch up with him. He invited me to go to a movie on Thursday night. I checked my schedule for parties. It would be an early night, so I figured we could do that.

The two days passed quickly. He came by at the end of work to take me to the movie. We were going to Cinema 1 and 2, which was a big deal then. It wasn't the downtown theater; it was the brand-new one. When we pulled up to the parking lot, there were easily three to four hundred young people waiting in line. I didn't know of any big box-office movies coming out or anything, and it was Thursday night, for goodness' sake.

We get out of the car, and I could instantly sense and hear them. They were Christians! The rage quickly rose inside me, and I clenched my right fist.

I was so mad at Stephen for tricking me. But I was all dressed up in my leisure suit and patent-leather boots. There was no way I could walk three miles back to my car. I was stuck.

He had gotten out of the car, not even looking my way. He knew I was mad, and he just went and got in line. The line went quickly into the movie theater, and we walked in to get our seats. He never said a word. He knew he had tricked me.

The movie was OK, about a young guy who'd had a rough time in life (hey, me too). At the end, he found God.

I was making money and having a good time. That God stuff, I didn't need or want. I stood up at the end, and I was going to walk out, but Stephen blocked me. He said (it was the first thing he said all night), "We are not done yet."

The tension was rising to a peak when luckily for both of us "the preacher" came on the movie screen. Remember, I had no church background and didn't know him, but you may have heard of him; his name was Billy Graham. His voice impacted me right away—not seeing him but hearing him. As I listened, I heard the meaning of that mysterious sign I had seen at football games on TV, John 3:16. I had never known what that was—maybe a crazy name or some kind of code? He quoted the verse. "For God so loved the world that He gave His only begotten Son, that whoever believes in Him should not perish but have everlasting life." That grabbed my attention like nothing before. At this point in my life, no one had ever said that he or she loved me. The first person I heard of who loved me was God. As the preacher continued, he told me that I could have peace in my life and be *part of the family* of God and that I had hope for eternal life with Him forevermore.

My heart was pounding out of my chest. It was the first time I'd heard those words, but for some reason, I knew they were true. When the preacher stopped speaking, he invited everyone to come down front to receive Jesus Christ as their Savior. I was so excited that I grabbed Stephen's arm and said, "Come on, man. We gotta go get saved."

Now remember, he and I were good friends at one time, so you can appreciate his next words. He looks at me and said, "You stupid idiot, I'm one of the church counselors. That's why I invited you to come. You need to bow on your knees right here in the popcorn, candy wrappers, and spilled Coke, repent from your sins, and ask Christ to forgive you and come into your life." He wouldn't even let me walk down the aisle.

We knelt, and we prayed, and I know that heaven came down, and glory filled my soul. I was now part of God's family forever. I got off my knees, knowing for the first time that somebody loved me, and it was God. That night, I knew Jesus as my Savior. He forgave me of my sins, He saved me from hell, and He gave me life everlasting. I can assure you that I am convinced of his love in my life every day. I've enjoyed His peace that passes all of our understanding. That's right. I'm part of the family of God. That's my story.

Has something like this ever happened to you? Was there ever a time in your life when you had a personal encounter with Jesus the Christ and asked Him to forgive you of your sins, and He saved you, and you now know you have eternal life?

TRUTH LEARNED—I'M SAVED
I *can* tell you it was real. I can guarantee you that it comforted me. It was so overwhelming. I knew something changed internally, and I loved it. This is different for everyone. Many know about the Bible or what some of it says but just haven't believed in it yet. They are way ahead of where I was. I knew nothing. But now, I believe everything.

I knew very little. They told me *I was saved*. That was, and still is, an interesting word, an extremely unusual word. *Saved*. Wow…but from what?

I was "saved" from the wrath of God. I didn't even know I was in trouble until that night. I heard that God was holy, and I was a sinner and we couldn't be together. That's why He had to make *hell* for all those who don't trust in Jesus. But now I'm *safe*. I won't go to hell. I'll never be separated from God—*ever*. The weight of the world fell off my back (although I'm not sure I was consciously aware of it). I later found out that the sin in my heart and life had been removed. I had a lighter walk. My sins, though many, had all been forgiven, cleansed, and washed away. I was and am *saved* from the wrath to come. And decades later, this is even more true to me than it was on that last Thursday in February 1975. At eight thirty on that evening, I was gloriously *saved*.

THE TEXT EMPHASIZED
JOHN 3:16 AND ACTS 4:12

There are many verses in the Bible that talk about how God loves us and wants to save all of us. You, me, and anyone in this world. I have picked two of them.

> "For God so loved the world that He gave His only begotten Son, that whoever believes in Him should not perish but have everlasting life."
> —John 3:16

There it is, that secret code I had seen on those signs so often but had no idea what it was or what it meant until that night. This verse is called the main theme of the whole Bible. All those books, chapters, and verses were written over fifteen hundred years ago by many different writers, and they are all saying (1) God does love us, and (2) He sent Jesus to save us from our sins, (3) so we could live forever with Him in heaven. What a deal—I couldn't refuse.

For God	*the greatest lover*
so loved	*the greatest degree*
the world	*the greatest company*
that He gave	*the greatest act*
His only begotten Son	*the greatest gift*
that whoever	*the greatest invitation*
believes	*the greatest simplicity*
in Him	*the greatest attraction*
should not perish	*the greatest promise*
but	*the greatest difference*
have	*the greatest certainty*
everlasting life	*the greatest possession*

This next passage is found in the book of Acts 4:12: "Nor is there salvation in any other, for there is no other name under heaven given among men by which we must be saved."

The backdrop of this verse is fascinating because when Peter and John used it, they were facing life or death. Many religious people didn't like Jesus. But with their personal convictions, even they when threatened with their very lives, Peter and John stood toe to toe, if you please, and said, "This is our story, and we are sticking to it...*period.*"

The rulers had no valid argument because Peter and John had just healed a lame man who had never walked. Everyone knew who the lame man was because they had seen him begging in front of the temple for years, and now he was up and running. How awesome! This verse, statement, even declaration is clear, and the message cannot be mistaken. There is no wiggle room or excuses. You believe in Him, or you don't. You are saved, or you are lost. God, the Bible, Jesus, and the disciples were very clear on this. I wanted to believe, and so I did, and just like the verse says, I was saved. *Wowzers.*

THE TITLE OF GOD AND ITS APPLICATION SAVIOR

Because of my past, I have a clear visual of the concept of "Savior." When I was going through all those awful life experiences, how nice it would have been to have had a Savior to come in and fix things. As children, we have parents, but I really didn't experience any of that kind of benefit. When I think of all the fights, bullies, gangs, and just plain thugs that came into my life, there were many, many times when someone or something came to my rescue. But there were also times when no additional help came, and I suffered the, we'll call it the lack of provision or protection, better known as pain.

But *now,* I had a Savior. It sounded sweet, safe, and secure. I did not know all the theology at the time, but when I thought of God, I pictured Him as my *savior,* my deliverer, my protector. And as the saying goes, "Lord knows I needed that."

Today, I can tell you all the theology stuff with great depth and complexity, but this really isn't the spot. I would like to share with you that only Christianity portrays salvation completely by the grace of a savior. Salvation comes exclusively and completely from God. All of salvation's resources come by grace from our savior and through faith in our savior. Contrary to all other religions of works, Christianity is a free gift from God.

I would like to leave you with just a few thoughts and verses to support the Bible's teaching about the "main theme." In the Old Testament, God is portrayed as Savior (Isa. 43:3, 11 45:15, 21, 22). In the New Testament, God is the only Savior (Jude 25 and, of course, Acts 4:12). And this Savior offers us all the hope and promise of eternal life (John 3:16, Matt. 1:21, Rom. 3:21–25, and many more).

I must mention the verses that I still hear ringing in my head, Romans 10:9, 10, 13, *"that if you confess with your mouth the Lord Jesus and believe in your heart that God has raised Him from the dead, you will be saved. For with the heart one believes unto righteousness, and with the mouth confession is made unto salvation. For whoever calls on the name of the Lord shall be saved."*

Now that's what I'm talking about! Jesus is the *Savior* of the world. When I think of God, I think of Him as my Savior.

THE THEOLOGICAL TEACHING APPLIED SALVATION

In my early walk with God, I often seemed to be confused about what the main point of the whole idea was. There was so much information, so many ideas, a to-do list, and a not–to-do list, and of course, the whens, wheres, whats, and whys. Let me summarize it all up for you and me. *It's all about Jesus. It's all about Jesus's work on the cross! It's all about Jesus's death, burial, and resurrection.* Let me hear an Amen.

Salvation is all about the Cross—that's all! When Paul wrote to the church in the city of Corinth, he laid it all out for us. First Corinthians 1:17, 18: The Cross is all you need for Salvation. First Corinthians 1:23, 24: Christ was crucified for all. First Corinthians 2:2: Christ crucified is all you need to know! Really that is it! Nobody before or after has ever done what Jesus did—nobody. That's why this is so awesome! That's why Jesus is more than a good teacher, more than a prophet, more than a good person. He is God's son, and He alone has conquered death, hell, and the grave and still lives forever more. Now that's not just me telling it; it's not just the Bible saying it. All of history has recorded it. At that time, there was not just "many" witnesses. There were the 12 disciples, the 120, and over 500 people who witnessed Jesus going up to heaven. And there are a lot more infallible proofs.

As I share this concept of salvation with you, I'd like to add some thoughts from Lewis Sperry Chafer's book *Systematic Theology Doctrine Summary on*

Salvation. In part, he explains so well the benefits of salvation in three tenses. Salvation has reference to the believer's past, present, and future:

1. The *past tense,* which releases us from the guilt and the penalty of sin, is wholly accomplished for all who believe at the time when they believe (Luke 7:50, 1 Cor. 1:18, 2 Cor. 2:15, 2 Tim. 1:9)
2. The *present tense,* which releases us from the power of sin, is being accomplished now in those who exercise faith for it (John 17:17; Rom. 6:14, 8:2; Gal. 5:16; Phil. 2:12–13)
3. The *future tense,* which releases us from the very presence of sin (Rom. 13:11; Eph. 5:25–27; Phil. 1:6; 1 Pet. 1:3–5; 1 John 3:1, 2)

If you take the time to comprehend the tremendous impact on your life, you'll never look back.

Maybe you know a lot about this "Bible stuff." I remember walking into a home-study group or to church knowing that everyone, and I mean *everyone,* knew more than I did about the Bible, church, Jesus, and the Christian walk. They all had been "doing it" for a while. But to me, it was brand new. This is my secret. I just believed it. I didn't doubt it, question it, or try to reason it out. I just believed it to be true and then claimed it as *mine.* Hey, God loves me. I'm forgiven of all my sins. (Wow, was that a miracle.) Was it blind faith? I don't think so. Was it arrogance? Trust me; I didn't have that much going on. But wait—I knew that. I knew I was saved because of what that preacher, Reverend Billy Graham, said was in the Bible. I *knew* that Jesus came into my heart that night, and I still know it today.

You now know my story, or at least the beginning. This was the first big—I'm telling you *huge* step—in not just turning my life around but also giving me everlasting life. I've got tears in my eyes right now thinking about it even after forty years. "Amazing Grace, how sweet the sound that saved a wretch like me."

You can have all this too! This may be a Defining Moment in your life that is really a Divine Appointment with God. Make it, take it, and do it. You'll never be sorry. All your sins can be washed away. You too can be cleansed from all that garbage in your life. Call upon Him. He is near, and He will rescue you, as He does with everyone who calls on Him.

Here is a simple prayer you can use to receive Jesus Christ as your Savior. It is just a suggested prayer. The exact wording doesn't matter; what counts is the attitude of your heart.

Lord Jesus, thank You for showing me how much I need You. Thank You for dying on the cross for me. Please forgive all my failures and the sins of my past. Help me to repent and turn from my sins. Make me clean and help me start fresh with You. I now receive You into my life as my Lord and Savior. Help me to love and serve You with all my heart. Amen.

Jesus said, "All that the Father gives Me will come to Me, and whoever comes to Me I will never cast out" John 6:37.

YOUR DESTINATION—A NEW BEGINNING

Becoming a Christian is only the beginning of your exciting journey. Jesus called it being "born again" (see John 3:3). It means that you now have a personal relationship with God as your heavenly Father. You are not alone.

THE TESTING OR TRIAL OF NOT TAKING THIS STEP

It's often hard to make a decision. When Benjamin Franklin had to make a big decision, he actually drew a line down the middle of a piece of paper and made a list of all the good on one side and all the bad on the other.

We have spent a great deal of time, space, and excitement sharing the good side of that paper. But what would be on the bad side if you chose to not accept Jesus as your Savior? Here is a simple list of consequences if you choose not to trust Jesus as your personal Savior. It is really much longer than this.

1. You will always have that nagging, empty *void* inside of you, that place in your soul that will always *ache* to be filled.
2. You will not personally experience how much God *loves* you, and He does *a lot*.
3. You won't know or understand how *close* God is. He's not just around you. He can be with you and *in* you always.
4. You won't get to experience the *help* He provides for being one of His children.
5. You won't know what it is like *working* with God and the plans He has here on earth.
6. You won't spend *eternity*—forever with Him.
7. You won't have the wonderful feeling of being completely made *new*.
8. You wouldn't have experienced *forgiveness* for your sins by God Himself, who paid for your sins.

Following are some verses that are affectionally called

THE ROMAN'S ROAD TO SALVATION—WHAT MUST I KNOW TO BE SAVED?

I. **The universal language** *charity = love*
"For God so loved the world that He gave His only begotten Son, that whoever believes in Him should not perish but have everlasting life" (John 3:16).

II. **The unfavorable lacking** *condemnation*
"As it is written: 'There is none righteous, no, not one for all have sinned and fall short of the glory of God'" (Rom. 3:10, 23).

III. **The unbelievable love** *commendeth* (demonstrated)
"But God demonstrates His own love toward us, in that while we were still sinners, Christ died for us" (Rom. 5:8).

IV. **The unconditional light** *compassion*

"For the wages of sin is death, but the gift of God is eternal life in Christ Jesus our Lord" (Rom. 6:23).

V. **The unique law** *confession*

"That if you confess with your mouth the Lord Jesus and believe in your heart that God has raised Him from the dead, you will be saved. For with the heart one believes unto righteousness and with the mouth confession is made unto salvation" (Rom 10:9–10).

VI. **The ultimate liberty** *calling*

"For whoever calls on the name of the Lord shall be saved" (Rom. 10:13).

VII. **The unlimited life** *conformation*

"I beseech you therefore brethren, by the mercies of God, that you present your bodies a living sacrifice, holy, acceptable to God, which is your reasonable service. And do not be conformed to this world, but be transformed by the renewing of your mind, that you may prove what is that good and acceptable and perfect will of God" (Rom. 12:1, 2).

Conclusion: Are you focused on other things of this world or on fancy Bible questions, or are you focused on the Cross of Calvary and what Jesus did for you? It's about the cross—that's all!

THE TRIBUTE SONG

As we all know, songs can simply "say it best." While there are dozens to choose from, this is one of my favorites.

"The Old Rugged Cross"
Rev. George Bennard

On a hill far away stood an old rugged cross,
The emblem of suffering and shame;
And I love that old cross where the dearest and best
For a world of lost sinners was slain.

Refrain

So, I'll cherish the old rugged cross,
Till my trophies at last I lay down;
I will cling to the old rugged cross,
And exchange it some day for a crown.

O that old rugged cross, so despised by the world,
Has a wondrous attraction for me;
For the dear Lamb of God left His glory above
To bear it to dark Calvary.

Refrain

In that old rugged cross, stained with blood so divine,
A wondrous beauty I see,
For 'twas on that old cross Jesus suffered and died,
To pardon and sanctify me.

Refrain

To the old rugged cross, I will ever be true;
Its shame and reproach gladly bear;
Then He'll call me some day to my home far away,
Where His glory forever I'll share.

Refrain

Just to name a few others to enjoy are:

"What Wondrous Love Is This?"

"At the Cross"

"There Is Power in the Blood"

6

HEY, BOY! WHO'S IN CHARGE?

I WANT TO tell you about the story, the moment, the appointment, the timing in my life, when I *knew* God was talking to me and about my next growth step.

The obvious first step is that we *must get saved*. We must begin with a forgiven life and the cleansing of Christ's blood. The rest of these Defining Moments, which very well may be Divine Appointments, can actually occur in any order that God chooses. But I have chosen to put them in this order because it shows a logical step-by-step process in our growth to be more like Jesus. We have to all remember that this is a spiritual process and not a rational one. God is in control...or is He? And we're not...or are we?

This brings us to the second step, and that's the topic of *surrender*.

It had been eight months since I had accepted Christ on that fateful evening in the movie theater, and I had just started going to church on Sunday mornings. My so-called mentor was the associate pastor. Every now and then, he would notice me, walk over, and give me a new, let's say, "suggestion," but it felt more like an "order." One Sunday morning he patted me on the back and said, "Hey, boy, don't you know we have church on Sunday nights? You should come." And that's how I started going to church on Sunday nights. For those of you who aren't southern, he wasn't using "boy" in a demeaning way. I was used to all the men in my family from South Carolina talking to me and others like that.

One evening, there was a large praise-and-worship group from Liberty Baptist College in the service. They were singing songs with an amazing message. You need to remember that I didn't know any church songs. I didn't even know "Jesus Loves Me." Until this time, I didn't know any gospel singers or Christian radio. I was listening to these young people (who were all about my age) sing such amazing messages from the Bible, and my heart started to stir inside of me again. It was like that first time in the movie theater when I got saved. I knew I was saved, but I didn't know what was going on inside me.

At the end of the evening, when they were giving the invitation (I knew what an invitation was now), I went forward by myself. The associate pastor was there, and he asked me, "What are you doing down here, boy?"

I stumbled about what to say; I really didn't know, and other people were coming down.

He pointed over to the corner of the altar and said, "Why don't you just pray over there, boy?"

Not really knowing how or what to pray, I started to share what was in my heart. I began with, "I know I'm saved, God. Thank you for loving me. But, God, I have this overwhelming impression that you want me to give everything to you. Not just my life, but all my plans and all my possessions. Lord, you know that my possessions aren't very many, and I certainly don't have any talents, but what I am and what I have, I'll give to you."

In other words, that night, I learned to *surrender* all to God. I didn't know I was supposed to do that before. He was my Savior, but that night, I learned that he was my Lord.

Over the next several weeks and months, I learned that a *surrendered life* requires sacrifice. Even Jesus said the same thing: "Not my will Father, but yours, be done." Sometimes the sacrifice was financial, sometimes it was time, and what little talents I had, they were all His. So in my Defining Moment on that Sunday night, eight months after my salvation, I learned to give it all at the altar…everything I was, everything I wanted to be, and everything I had was *surrendered* to God. Everything I am is His. That evening over in the corner of the church's altar, surrounded by so many people at the altar getting saved, I was having a clear conversation with God Himself. *Wow.* It was amazing! He not only loved me but also wanted me. I learned that because He had given His all, I should do the same. My "all" wasn't much, but I gave Him all of me—everything! I was happily nervous to do it. Remember I have been taking care of things all by myself since I was fifteen. But now, wow, what a relief it was, knowing how much God loved me and that He wanted all of me (dirt, baggage, and all). Another burden had been lifted. Praise the Lord!

THE TRUTH LEARNED—SACRIFICE

I'll never forget the night when I was preaching in Cuba to about three hundred college-age kids. It was their church, and they were all fired up. We didn't even start until nine, but they weren't in a hurry. Announcements, prayer requests (we just about had revival during that prayer time), and worship. Praise God, I was just so blessed, and once again, that "heart to heart" that I've gotten addicted to, that presence of God, was there! And it was stirring in my heart again (thank you, Lord). My sermon topic was *surrender.*

I told them, we are American, and we don't surrender to anyone…period. Yet here I am, sharing with you about how on earth I got here…from there, and one of the most important steps is to *surrender.* But surrender to God doesn't mean like we picture, to wave the white flag and give up. Yes, it does involve all of that, but it includes one more step: transferring control and leadership to another. I have chosen the Lord Jesus Christ to be in charge of my life—everything. I gave Him everything I was and had. It might not be much, but He wanted it.

While I was preaching to the awesome young people in Cuba, I got to the point in the message where our human nature fights this surrender process. "No," we say. "I want to be in charge. No, I don't know what He might want of me. I don't want to give up this or that." And on and on we go.

Out of the blue, I was overwhelmed remembering what else He had done for me when I surrendered to Him my everything. As I was preaching, God was reminding me of many things that I had given Him that He gladly took and cleaned up, and I shared them with these young Christians in Cuba.

Yes, I did give God all that I was, all that I had, and all my plans. But remember, my "everything" included all the hatred in my heart. He took it and gave me love. He took all the meanness in my life and gave me peace. He took all the frustration in my life and gave me joy. From all the sins in my being, He cleansed me and gave me forgiveness, freedom, and liberty. And like that Sunday night at the corner of the altar, the chains *fell off* in every area of my life. When I surrendered to God, I was *not* captured and tortured. I was cleaned up, made whole, and set free.

I know I'm supposed to be talking about the truth that I learned, and it was sacrifice, which can be another horrible word picture, especially when you combine it with surrendering. Who on earth wants to do that? Yes, to serve God, I had to change my friends, but He has given me real friends now. He changed the places I went, and those places are all more fun and meaningful. Oh yes, He did change my life! How indescribable this journey has been! I could not have even dreamed that it could be so. Now God and I are asking you to give up—yes, give in. Absolutely. Give it all completely. Give it all to God. Don't you think that the God of the universe and, let me remind you, your Creator, can do a lot better with you than you can?

It's a sacrifice of your life that will reap so many unbelievable, positive benefits and blessings in your life. Yes, His plans are unknown, and it can be uncomfortable. But it is worth the wait, without a doubt. What appears to be a great cost or sacrifice will be your greatest success.

THE TEXT EMPHASIZED
ROMANS 12:1

I hope, I pray, I beg you, I plead with all of my heart, mind, body, and soul that with the help of the Holy Spirit, I can help you understand this one verse. This is "just" one verse in the whole Bible, so what's the big deal? That's the point; it's a really big deal.

After living the Christian life for decades now, it's obvious, it's sad, it's heartbreaking, and it's frustrating to watch and hear Christians get *stuck*. This is a primary theme throughout the Bible, but here in Romans 12:1, it's all summed up, and it's perfectly clear. You do it, or you don't. And I know most didn't—don't. The huge problem in the churches today is spiritual immaturity. Christians aren't grown up. They aren't even growing a little. So much is faked. We've all heard about those "hypocrites" at church. Well, sometimes it's true, isn't it?

I know God is talking to us, saying, "Come on, my children; please grow up just a little. And if you take the first few steps, you just don't have any idea what I have in store for your life. It's amazing! But come on, kids; take this step. Plenty have done it, and they have all been *happy* they did!"

Are you curious? What's the step, Lord? It's called surrender or consecration of the Lordship of Christ or, most simply put, "Who is in charge of your life, you or God?" Romans 12:1 says it best: "I beseech you therefore, brethren, by the mercies of God, that you present your bodies a living sacrifice, holy, acceptable to God, which is your reasonable service."

If you are saved and you know it, say "Amen." If you're saved and you know it, that's sometimes called "fire insurance." The Christian walk here on earth is a whole lot more than just being saved. It's about growth, and it all starts here. Listen. "I beg you, I plead with you, I beseech you." Please, hear me on this! God is so merciful to you, He was so good to you, He has forgiven you, and He knows he can do more with your life than you can. *But* He won't *take* it by force; it's your life. You have to *give* Him your life and even present it to God as a "living sacrifice."

I know it seems like a big step when you are little. It's not really that big a step, but it is a big deal! Go ahead. Give God your body, your talent, your time, your treasures. That's your head, feet, hands, eyes, ears, breath, heart, mind. You are all in. "I beseech you," Paul said. I beg of you. Your life will change and grow. You can't even imagine, but please go ahead and be obedient to God. Trust Him. He has great plans for you if you let Him. It is up to you.

Let me ask you a question. Really, how is it working for you? Do you feel God's power and His presence often? Are you aware of His plans and purpose? This may be the Defining Moment in your life that may be a Divine Appointment. Go ahead and *surrender* to *him*.

THE TITLE OF GOD AND ITS APPLICATION
LORD = LORDSHIP OF CHRIST

When we want to take the next step in Christ, to follow Him and be transformed to His likeness, we have to consider Him Lord—Lord of all. He now means more to you than Savior "fire insurance." This new relationship is finally recognizing Him as Lord of your life—everything.

- "When Jesus comes on the scene and begins His ministry, we find He is Lord of the Sabbath" (Luke 6:5).
- "He is the Lord Christ of Israel" (1 Cor. 8:6).
- "We only have the awareness and ability to call Him Lord by the leading of the Holy Spirit" (1 Cor. 12:3).

- "Once we have and recognize that 'Defining Moment' that is a 'Divine Appointment' then and only then will we recognize Him as Lord over all" (John 3:31).
- "He is Lord of both the dead and the living" (Rom. 14:9).
- "Which makes Him head of the church" (Col. 1:18)
- "Even greater than Moses" (Heb. 3:3).

And finally, you'll see Him as the Alpha and Omega (Rev. 1:11). The first and the last, not just of the churches but also of our lives. It's called surrender. The truth that I learned in the process is *sacrifice*. First, I "gave up" everything for Him. Then I "gave him" everything, and last, "I got" tremendous relief and freedom because of the sacrifice. In other words, "I gave it all on the altar. It seemed like a big sacrifice, but it was nothing compared to what He did. That's a *big deal*.

THE THEOLOGICAL TEACHING APPLIED SURRENDER

Hey, I get it. *Surrender* is nobody's favorite word. But God considers it to be the place where we enter into the heart of worship. I hear it, and I see it. We all want to live out our own lives on our own terms. Let me be frank, that is not godly living. That's godless living. There have been many books written about taking up your cross or dying to self, making Jesus Lord of your life, and consecration to God. But how do we do those things? A preacher of the last century, A. W. Tozer, said, "The reason why many are still troubled, still seeking, still making little forward progress is because they have not yet come to the end of themselves. We're still trying to give orders and interfering with God's work within us." I'd suggest reading it again until you get it.

Let me explain it a little differently. A surrendered life means these four principles:

1. *Following* God's lead *without knowing where* He is sending you.
2. *Waiting* for God's timing *without knowing when* it will come.

3. *Expecting* a miracle *without knowing how* God will provide it.
4. *Trusting* God's purpose *without understanding* the circumstances.

"Surrender yourself to the Lord and wait patiently for Him" (Ps. 37:7a).

- Surrender does not mean a conversion or a state of sinless perfection.
- Surrender is not necessarily a sudden impulse or emotion developed in excitement.
- Surrender is simply the soul trusting wholly in Jesus—no holding back in reserves.
- It is giving ourselves up to Christ forever, as bought with a price; we are no longer our own.

SEVEN PRINCIPLES OF SURRENDER (EXTRA CREDIT)

I want to continue by covering seven principles about surrender.

1. **What Is Surrender?**
   I think we have covered it pretty well, but I want to add one more thought. It is me yielding my will to God—and God's acceptance of my offering. *Praise the Lord.*
2. **Who Can Surrender?**
   Anybody at any time who is in the body of Christ. Anyone who has been cleansed by the blood of Jesus.
3. **The Appeal to Surrender**
   We are not commanded to come by force. We are to think about how merciful God has been, remembering that we have been redeemed, that we are His children, that there is no more condemnation, that He gives us heaven and the Holy Spirit, and the list goes on and on. Why not surrender?

4. **The Act of Surrender**

   It is *voluntary*. We must choose to do it. With me and my moment at the altar, I had to surrender because I wanted to please my Savior and wanted to obey and follow him.

   It is *personal*. It's you, your body. Nobody else is involved. I was OK being off in the corner. Hey, I was meeting with God!

   It is *sacrificial*—a living (continual) sacrifice, a daily, ongoing, continual putting our lives on the altar.

5. **What Am I to Surrender?**

   Ha! Everything! All the rooms in your house of life. You give God your body, your time, your talents and treasures, and most importantly, your whole heart.

6. **The Argument for a Surrendered Life**

   It's reasonable. That's what God said, and Billy Sunday, the most famous evangelist of the early twentieth century, said, "God's service is not unreasonable. It is the only sensible thing to do." Who do you think can do a better job with your life, you or God?

7. **The Results of a Surrendered Life**

   Let me just name a few. You will be less worldly and selfish; your friends and family will like that. You'll have more internal values and be less materialistic. You'll be happier, just for being obedient to God. You'll be more able to "accept" life as it is. You'll feel more beneficial, happy, and victorious. You can see the list could go on and on. Oh, His abundant mercies!

My final thought on this is that with surrender, you take the Big Step (Rom. 12:1). After that, it's an ongoing process. It's not like we ever achieve it (though I must admit we do have moments when we are truly in tune with God). It's an ongoing dependence and an intimate relationship with God that help you grow you every day to be more like His Son.

Wouldn't you like to have that someday? It's worth anything and everything you give up—I know!

THE TESTING OR TRIAL OF NOT TAKING THIS STEP

If you choose, as a Christian, not to surrender to the Lordship of Jesus Christ, here are a few of the blessings you will *not* experience:

- You likely will not know the will of God in your life.
- Your material things and wants will grow unsatisfying.
- You will likely "feel" like you are not finished—or complete in Him.
- You will likely not experience the full power of God in your life very often.
- Your self-rule will frustrate the will and power of God in your life (grieve the Holy Spirit).

This is by no means a complete or absolute list. But I must ask you, is it worth (whatever it is you are hanging on to) to not have the direction of God in your life? And then not knowing if you are living in God's will? It is the next step in the spiritual walk that gets you closer to knowing what God's will for your life is. Why not make today that Defining Moment, that Divine Appointment, and surrender your all to him…Amen.

PRAYER OF SURRENDER

Loving Father, I surrender to You today with all my heart and soul. Please come into my heart in a deeper way. I say, "Yes" to you today. I open all the secret places of my heart to You and say, "Come on in." Jesus, you are the Lord of my whole life. I believe in you and receive you as my Lord and Savior. I hold nothing back. Holy Spirit, bring me to a deeper conversion to the person of Jesus

Christ. I surrender all to you: my time, my treasures, my talents, my health, my family, my resources, my work, my relationships, my time management, my successes, and my failures. I release it, and let it go. I surrender my understanding of how things "ought" to be, my choices, and my will. I surrender to you the promises I have kept and the promises I have failed to keep. I surrender my weaknesses and strengths to you. I surrender my emotions, my fears, my insecurities, my sexuality. I especially surrender _____

_____

_____

(Continue to surrender other areas as the Holy Spirit reveals them to you.) Lord, I surrender my whole life to you: the past, the present, and the future. In sickness and in health, in life and in death, I belong to you.

Take me, Lord, and receive all my memory, my understanding, and my entire will with all that I have and possess. You have given me all that I have, O Lord, and I return it. All is Yours. Dispose of it wholly according to Your will. Give me Your love and Your grace, for this is sufficient for me.

Amen.

If you prayed this prayer and meant it…tell a friend and if you don't mind, email me at Jimwillisbooks@gmail.com to tell me your exciting news.

THE TRIBUTE SONG

"I Surrender All"
Judson W. VanDeVenter
Music: Winfied S. Weeden

All to Jesus I surrender,
All to Him I freely give;
I will ever love and trust Him,
In His presence daily live.

> *Refrain*
> I surrender all,
> I surrender all;
> All to Thee, my blessed Savior,
> I surrender all.

All to Jesus I surrender,
Humbly at His feet I bow;
Worldly pleasures all forsaken,
Take me, Jesus, take me now.

All to Jesus I surrender,
Make me, Savior, wholly Thine;
Let me feel the Holy Spirit,
Truly know that Thou art mine.

All to Jesus I surrender,
Lord, I give myself to Thee;
Fill me with Thy love and power,
Let Thy blessing fall on me.

7

A Fifth or a Case?

As we are studying how on earth I got here…from there, the obvious first step is that we have to be saved. I had been saved for four to five months when my friend Stephen—who invited me to the movies—threw a Bible onto the front seat of the car and told me that I needed to *read the Bible*. I never read much, and I wasn't a very good reader. So to pick up a book that was three fingers thick, now that was completely intimidating. Nevertheless, I set up a time to read. On my first "Bible-reading night," I got home to my singles-only apartment complex, and Wally, across the hallway, was having a party. Ah, temptation, but no, I was going to read. I grabbed a couple of beers and sat them beside my beanbag chair and turned on my music. I plopped down, contemplating how in the world I would read this book.

I distinctly remember opening the Bible and looking at the table of contents. I noticed two things right off the bat. There were a lot of strange titles. What in the world is a Deuteronomy? Who in the world is Ecclesiastes? What's a Corinthians and why do they need two of them? The next thing I noticed was that most of the books were really, really long. So, I closed it again, relaxed, listened to music, and drank a beer. I was trying to figure out how in the world I would ever get started, when I had an idea. I'd just open it up, and wherever it fell, I would start from there. I thought, "Well, I can do that," so I put it in my lap, put my fingers in the pages, and popped it open to the book of what I saw as "Pro-verbs." I began right where I looked, chapter 20, and I started reading the first verse. I read, "Wine is a mockery and strong drink is raging and whosoever is deceived thereby is not wise." Have you ever been hit in the stomach and not been prepared?

I was thinking so that's the Bible? "Where's Jesus? Where is that love of God stuff? Where is that 'peace' that the preacher was talking about?" The first thing I thought about was at least it didn't say beer. I just sat there for I don't know how long. I looked at the verse again, and I closed the Bible. As a little footnote, I didn't remember what that reference was. I didn't find it for another year or two. But as I sat there, I realized that God wanted me to stop drinking. I had been drinking four cases of beer a week for three or four years, and He wanted me to stop.

I finished the beers I had out, and I said, "OK, I'll do it." I had three six-packs in the fridge, and I took them over to Wally's party. I probably owed them to him anyway, and I left them. I hung out for just a minute but actually felt uncomfortable. I left and went back to my apartment across the hall.

Have you ever been involved in a chain letter? Supposedly they don't work, but it seems like everybody talks about them and has done at least one. Well, I had gotten involved in something like a chain letter three days earlier. I gave the people on the list phone calls and asked them if they wanted me to buy them a fifth or a case of beer. Then I wrote five names down and mailed the same request to them. I got the letter, and again, I probably owed this guy a case of beer anyway, so I filled out the chain letter and completely forgot about it until the next day. I went to work at my dad's clothing store, and all day long I was getting phone calls. "Hey, Jim, I'm in this chain letter. Do you want a fifth or a case of beer?" People knew I drank beer, and they kept dropping it off at the store, all day long.

Remember that *I had just quit drinking the night before, right?* By the end of the day, I had *eight cases of beer* sitting next to the cash register in my dad's clothing store. It was at that time in my young Christian life (I'd only been saved for four to five months) that I realized there was spiritual warfare.

Obviously, Dad had a few questions. My father's clothing store was a specialty boutique of men's and women's clothing called Pacer's. We served cocktails to help customers relax, look around, and feel comfortable. What in the world would I do with eight cases of beer? I didn't drink anymore, so I decided to give them to my dad to use for stock in the store. That created a lot of unsaid words, thoughts, and impressions between us. When I told my dad that I had been saved, he had a mixed response. "OK son, that's nice, but don't get too wrapped up in it." That was the beginning of the "quiet conflict."

The topic we are talking about right now is *separation*. I had learned the night before that God was asking me to *separate from my worldly lifestyle*. Not just the drinking but also all the worldly relationships that I had. I didn't know what that was yet, but I knew he wanted me to act differently. Remember, I had *just read one verse* in the Bible for the first time. I understood God to be not just my Savior, not just my Lord but also "the Holy One." He wanted me to be like Him, and I wasn't. I didn't know what the repercussions would be with this decision, but I sensed it was going to create *solitude*. And it certainly did. It put a wall up between my dad and me. Obviously, I couldn't hang out with everybody at the parties at the singles-only complex and all the activity that surrounded me there.

So the concept of *solitude* in this new relationship with the Holy One... has something like this ever happened to you?

THE TRUTH TO BE LEARNED—SOLITUDE

I'm an *extrovert*. I am really out there. I have to tone it down on an ongoing basis. I've learned that not everybody is like me. Actually, there are very few. When I do run into them, it's a blast. It's crazy; it's fun! On every one of those "personality" tests, I am off the page as an extrovert. When I see introverts—and, oh my, there are plenty of them—I can also see how painful I can be to them. Wow, I must really work at toning it down, Jimbo.

So let's talk about this *truth to be learned—solitude*. The Bible uses the phrase "set apart unto a holy purpose." For me, it was very hard, very obvious, and very uncomfortable. Again, introverts would have been fine with solitude, but not me! *Solitude,* by definition, is "the state of being or living alone." There was nothing—I mean nothing—in my life that I wanted to do alone… nothing at all. I always crave having people around me. I strived for it, and I got it. But this solitude thing, "the quality of being or feeling lonely or deserted, isolated, feeling detached"—*yikes.* I knew all about that, living in the tree in the woods years ago. I didn't want any more of that. But boy, change was coming, and it came fast and hit hard.

My dad knew something had happened to me. Remember that every night we finished the day having a couple of drinks to relax and recount the day. But now I was having a *Coke.* Can I say awkward? And during store hours, I wasn't as free as I used to be in offering a drink to our customers, and that bothered him on another level as well—money. So let's just say things got a little sticky.

Then there was where I lived, partied, hung out with friends, and the crazy activities…*everywhere, all the time.* Wowzers! I had to stay away and not be found or seen. What was I going to say, "Yeah, man, I found God" like Stephen did? Oh my, that was just too corny. Or what about, "Hey, guys, I quit drinking." I'd be a laughingstock on so many levels! Why would I do that anyway? I was having a lot of fun.

Let's pause for a moment. Here's a confession: I did love to drink. I did have fun. And I couldn't wait to do it again the next day. I loved it. But one night, in reading *the first verse I ever read in the Bible,* of all things, I knew loud and clear that God was asking me to quit drinking—even though it didn't say beer. (Ha-ha.)

So there I was, right smack dab in the middle of a party city, knowing all the people. Oh, and might I add I was right smack in the middle of my lease too. I had nowhere to go. I was stuck in the world of parties. I did my best to stay out of sight. I encountered plenty of people, and of course, they asked a few questions. Thankfully, nobody got obnoxious, yet several had no problem with laughing at me. I knew that at one time, I would have too. I badly needed something else to do—and soon!

I tried to hang out with some of those Christians. I felt that so many of them were clueless about things, but I did attach to a couple of people who seemed to be more like me in certain ways. I went to different events put on by churches, but what kept me really busy and involved was going to these home Bible studies. Wow. I could go learn about the Bible without having to read it. Cool.

The point is that when I let go of all my old ways and old friends, there was definitely a time of loneliness and solitude, and even a separation in my relationship with Dad. But I was able to fill that emptiness with new church friends and new activities, and this was the beginning of a new lifestyle in Christ.

My world changed *for the better.* It was the beginning of a lifelong change called *transformation.*

THE TEXT EMPHASIZED
ROMANS 12:2 AND 2 CORINTHIANS 6:14–17

"And do not be conformed to this world, but be transformed by the renewing of your mind, that you may prove what is that good and acceptable and perfect will of God" (Romans 12:2).

This verse and verse one, which we have already talked about, are popular verses. They are quoted all the time. I guess it's because they flow out so easily. Maybe it's because they're a little poetic. But the concepts of "conformed to this world" and "being transformed" are huge topics. And to tell you the truth, it can get dirty here! And it can get ugly with some of our family and friends. In some places in the world, I've seen people get kicked out of their villages, removed from their families, and even killed because they believed in Jesus Christ and wanted to live out a different life. *Are you ready for this?* God is and will be with you all the way if you choose to be obedient to Him and take on this growth step. Your world will change! So get ready for the *renewing of your mind* like nothing you have ever imagined. What is so cool and so exciting is that it's happening every day, all over the world. Why not with you?

There are a lot of excuses. There are lots of fears and unknowns, but hey, you already gave God control of everything in the last chapter on surrender, right? So what's the big deal?

THE DETAILS

"Do not be unequally yoked together with unbelievers. For what fellowship has righteousness with lawlessness? And what communion has light with darkness? And what accord has Christ with Belial? Or what part has a believer with an unbeliever? And what agreement has the temple of God with idols? For you are the temple of the living God. As God has said: 'I will dwell in them And walk among them. I will be their God, And they shall be My people.' *Therefore Come out from among them And be separate, says the Lord. Do not touch what is unclean, And I will receive you*" (2 Cor. 6:14–17).

This concept of *unequally yoked* is easy to comprehend—it's just hard to do. Maybe we don't want to believe it is that important and that it would make that big of a difference. But God thinks it does, and if He thinks it is important to you then *you* should think it is important to you. It's just about obeying God. Oh, there's one of those "details" again. The Holy One doesn't want you to be around those places, doing those things, and hanging out with these people. Why? Simply because it's not good for you. It won't help you grow.

We have all heard that growing up is hard to do, but it matters. By the way, as hard as it was (and I'll admit it was), it was ten times more rewarding. I reaped the benefits physically, mentally, socially, and especially spiritually. So much bondage and chains and self-destructive habits came to an end. Peace and a clear conscience with the power of God are daily possessions. I want to keep these—what about you?

THE WRONG WAY

"Do not love the world or the things in the world. If anyone loves the world, the love of the Father is not in him. For all that is in the world—the lust of the flesh, the lust of the eyes, and the pride of life—is not of the Father but is of the world. And the world is passing away, and the lust of it; but he who does the will of God abides forever" (1 John 2:15–17).

We could call this passage "The Love That God Hates." It really doesn't take a rocket scientist to figure this out (although listening to scientists today, most have not). This world is a mess. It's getting worse all the time. It's sad, but it is. I'm not saying that there isn't a lot of fun stuff to do. But this "world" I'm speaking of is spiritually dark. Many, many things do not glorify God and His holy character. God doesn't want us to love the worldly behaviors. His creation is awesome, isn't it? But that's not what we're talking about. As Christians, this is no longer our home. We are just passing through. We now have a much better place set aside for us. Let's make those plans.

THE WHY

"Or do you not know that your body is the temple of the Holy Spirit who is in you, whom you have from God, and you are not your own? For you were bought at a price; therefore, glorify God in your body and in your spirit, which are God's" (1 Cor. 6: 19–20).

When I first read these words, the spirit inside of me just broke down with gratefulness, disbelief, and joy. I'm a temple of God. And then I started thinking about what Jesus did for me on the cross, and I was compelled to respond to Him with joyful obedience and to say to God, "What do you want me to do? Thank you for loving me so. How can I possibly show my love back to you?" I live knowing that I belong to God Almighty, the Holy One. Who would have ever thought? How did I get here?

THE TITLE OF GOD APPLIED—HOLY ONE

Wowzers! This is just about impossible for me to cover right here. It is particularly impossible for us to comprehend. *My God,* the God of the Bible, has so many awesome characteristics. One of these characteristics is that He is Holy. We read in Exodus 15:11, "Who is like You, O Lord, among the gods? Who is like You, glorious in holiness, Fearful in praises, doing wonders?" Also, in 1 Samuel 6:20, "Who is able to stand before this holy Lord God? And to whom shall it go up from us?" and in Psalms 99:9, "Exalt the Lord our God, and worship at His holy hill; For the Lord our God is holy."

> Let me share just a couple more verses. "And one cried to another and said: 'Holy, holy, holy is the Lord of hosts; The whole earth is full of His glory!'" (Isa. 6:3).

In Revelations, read the entire chapters of four and five. Amazing *Holy* God. Here's just one more quote: "The four living creatures, each having six wings, were full of eyes around and within. And they do not rest day or night, saying: "Holy, holy, holy, Lord God Almighty, Who was and is and is to come!" (Rev. 4:8). No, this is not science fiction! It's real. It's happening now and in heaven, the holy place.

This is just a sampling of the references that talk about the *holiness of God.* All these and more became, let's say, more visible, when I begin to *separate* my life from the world. This whole new identity of God (to me) started pulling back the curtains in this area of my life so much so that I realized I have a responsibility to respond to that *holiness*. It's absolutely true that God loves you just where you are, but He doesn't want to keep you there. That's why *separation* is such an important growth step in your life and mine. It unquestioningly alters, well, everything.

Just this one subject *Holy One, holiness* is so huge that even part of His person, the Holy Spirit, is a complete character throughout all creation. The beginning of the nation of Israel and the entire books of the Bible, Exodus and Leviticus, talk about the *Holiness of the Lord* and give great detail to building a tabernacle with the *Holy of Holies*. God's serious about this, and it's obvious that a lot of believers in the church are *not concerned* with having a *holy life.*

But God is holy, and *He wants us to be holy.* In Peter 1:16, the Bible goes on and on (and I will try not to here) revealing the holiness of God and encourages us to be holy too. In Luke 1:74–75, "To grant us that we, being delivered from the hand of our enemies, Might serve Him without fear, In holiness and righteousness before Him all the days of our life." Again, in 2 Corinthians 7:1, "Therefore, having these promises, beloved, let us cleanse ourselves from all filthiness of the flesh and spirit, perfecting holiness in the fear of God."

Whew! We have many examples in both the Old and New Testaments, and then, of course, the perfect example is our Lord, Jesus Christ. Let's be like him. Simple, right?

THE THEOLOGICAL TEACHING OF SEPARATION
Other words used for separation are consecration, holiness, being "in Christ," transformed, a follower, and so on.

This topic is highly controversial. And I want to be clear that it is also very individualistic, which only makes it more complicated. There are many things that God *doesn't* want us doing, and there are many things He *does* want us to do. Since we the church people are all at different levels of maturity in our walks, it looks all the more confusing. There are so many personal feelings and experiences that enter this topic. It's quite volatile, explosive, and, may I add at great danger, *selfish.*

You can call it whatever you want, but it is really all about this: Who? What? When? Where? Why?

Do you want to be more like God or not?

Do you want to be strong in the Lord or not?

Do you want to act more like heaven or hell?

All our emotional stories, excuses, preferences, and personal cravings are just hooks into the world that won't let us be released from (OK, here we go; I'm going to say it) *sin.* I'm going to take it one step further. If you are so determined to keep the questionable "thing" in your life, period, then maybe it has grown into an "idol" before God. Sit back and think about that.

The fact that you or I am arguing with God is quite humorous or sad. Maybe it's just stupid. Yes, I said that word too. Look, think about it. This whole concept of *separation* is for our benefit, and yet, we, me, you fight it like the dickens! We, I, you want to cling to these precious who, what, when, where, and why knowing that they are not the best for us. They aren't even "acceptable for us" (important injector), but I'll be darned if I'm ever going to let this go. It's me; it's mine!

All God is trying to get you to do is let go. Just let it go, my dear child, and I'll give you something that you want and need that will be so much better. God says, "Trust me—nobody loves you more than I do. Nobody wants you to be happier than I do. Nobody wants you to go further in life than I do. Let it go…I have something else that is so much better! But I can't give it to you until you let go. Come on…let's go."

This is a Defining Moment that's clearly a Divine Appointment. You hear that voice. You feel that pressure. You know exactly what God is asking you to do. Right now is the time to just agree with God and trust Him completely. Give it up. Let go and let God! Fall before Him, turn away from your worldly ways, and follow him. Follow him again into that next growth step, *separation* from the world to God. Do it now; I'll wait for you.

Crazy, right? I hope you get used to it. God loves to talk to his children. That's so cool. I love it. God wants to talk to me and to you. To make the step work, you're going to have to want to talk to God a lot. You want to pray to him more for strength and encouragement. You need to read His book, the Bible, a lot more. It is here that you will find the strength and the will to stand your new ground and decide to never go back. Just don't do it. Period. Done.

You see in *regeneration*, our nature changes;
In *justification*, our standing is changed;
In *adoption*, our position is changed;
and, in *separation*, our character is changed.

By the way, separation is a two-step process. You separate yourself *from* sin, and then *to* God. In the Bible, the holy life and being separated is mentioned over a thousand times! Do you think it's important to God? You bet it is. Separation shows the fruit of a justified life.

Let me give a simple yet helpful illustration. I've done several funerals. Some are people I know well, and some I don't. Unless you have given your family and friends an abundance of evidence that you are saved, it makes the funeral hard, uncomfortable, and awful. But if you have truly been living for Christ and not for yourself, it will easily be known that you are a follower and someone who is "saved," safe from hell and on your way to heaven. Yep, much nicer. So help us preachers out, will ya?

I have covered a lot of Bible teaching in this chapter already, but I want to give you a few helpful hints. God uses five things to help us transform and separate.

1. The Word of God (John 17:17)
    To be cleansed, we need to spend much time with God's word; it purifies and separates us.
2. By the blood of Christ (Heb. 13:12)
    The Word reveals sin; the blood cleanses it away. The result is separation.
3. By chastisement (Heb. 12:10)
    Those who have had kids knows that they need corrections every now and again—well, all the time!
4. By yielding to God (Rom. 6:19)
    Actually, the whole chapter should be studied regularly.
5. By ourselves (2 Cor. 7:1)

There are a lot of things that God has already done for us, and there are a lot of things that Jesus does for us. And the Holy Spirit does so much too and helps here in this topic. But you and I need to take ownership here. We are greatly involved. We too have a part in separation; our part is seeking out the sin, judging it, casting it away, and praying for strength to live a holy life.

We need to claim Christ in our lifestyle daily. Also, please remember that I began this chapter stating that this is *very individualistic,* and I want to end it that way. Do what God wants *you* to do. He is working on everyone else too.

TESTING OR TRIALS IF THE STEP IS NOT TAKEN

If you choose not to *separate* yourself from the world as a Christian, these are blessings you will not experience and some frustrations you will continue to experience:

- You will always be defending yourself to God.
- You probably won't understand God's will in your life.
- The baggage of worldliness, sin will be your constant burden.
- You may have feelings of not fitting in around God's family.
- Guilt will likely be a good friend—not the kind you want though.
- God will continually "bother you" about your position.
- You will likely receive some criticism from some of the church family. Sorry. Some think it's their job.

Again, it's not an exhaustive list here. If you haven't separated to God yet, you might be able to add to the list, so e-mail me some of your additional experiences at JimWillisBooks@gmail.com.

THE TRIBUTE SONG

"I Have Decided to Follow Jesus"
Source: unknown
Melody arranged by Eugene Thomas

I have decided to follow Jesus;
I have decided to follow Jesus;
I have decided to follow Jesus;
No turning back, no turning back.
I have decided to follow Him.

The world behind me, the cross before me;
The world behind me, the cross before me;
The world behind me, the cross before me;
No turning back, no turning back.
I have decided to follow Him.

Though none go with me, still I will follow;
Though none go with me, still I will follow;
Though none go with me, still I will follow;
No turning back, no turning back.
I have decided to follow Him.

Will you decide now to follow Jesus?
Will you decide now to follow Jesus?
Will you decide now to follow Jesus?
No turning back, no turning back.
I have decided to follow Him.

8

TO GO OR NOT TO GO –
ARE YOU KIDDING ME?

Two and a half years after Stephen had "tricked" me into going to the movies where I got saved, it was obvious that God was leading me to attend Bible college. It seemed like a big stretch for me in so many ways, such as my problems with reading, difficulties with studying, where to live, and finances. Well, when it came to the finances, I was going completely on faith. It seemed like every month, I came up short and had to meet with the bookkeeper to figure out how I was going to pay the college.

In December, once again, I was called into the college bookkeeper's office because I hadn't paid all my rent and tuition. Since it was the end of the semester, she mentioned that I wouldn't get my report card if I wasn't paid in full. I asked her, "Do I have to have a report card?"

With a surprised look on her face, she said, "Why, no, you don't need a report card."

So I said, "OK, then let's give God time to provide."

The first thing that happened was during the Christmas break. It snowed and snowed. To me, it was big time. Sixteen inches was a lot. I had only seen snow twice in my life, and none of it was like this. So I decided that I'd shovel snow to make some money. Everyone thought I was nuts. Well, surprise. I walked up to a house not far from the college and knocked on the door to offer my services, and a little old couple was thrilled. Here it was, just my second time in snow, and I was in the snow shoveling business. When I got through, a neighbor asked if I would do theirs. They all determined the price because I told them I had no idea what to charge but needed the money for my family. They were such a blessing. I never even got off that block—almost everyone hired me. In those two days, I did twelve to fifteen driveways and sidewalks by myself. Funny! Remember my dad's clothing store-in Florida? The only winter clothing I had was a London Fog topcoat with a ski hat, jeans, and work boots. I was funny looking and frozen, but I earned a lot of cash.

About a month later, a grocery-store strike came about, and I still had no job and no money, but I still had these responsibilities. So I made some phone calls. I worked it out with the store to come in (if I could get in), and they would put me to work. I drove through and broke the picket line. It was scary and dangerous, but the needs of my wife and child were more important.

It was a Friday afternoon. The store stock was in shambles, and I was supposed to stock the shelves. Other than ten minutes of quick training, I was left to my duties. I worked hard into the night. Nobody seemed to be looking for me or needing me, so I just kept stocking empty shelves on and on into the night.

The new manager for the Saturday shift came in, and we got caught up and updated. He asked if I was OK. I mentioned that I was hungry. He got the deli to cook me a great breakfast and asked me how long I want to work. I said, "As long as I can," and he agreed. So I continued all Saturday as well.

There must've been a stir going on outside all weekend—some increased tension and hollering—and the police, TV news, and so on were there. The Saturday-night shift manager came in and said, "You're still here, Willis?"

I said, "Yes sir. Is that OK?"

"Oh yes but take a break." He sent me over to the deli, and they fed me again. What marveled everyone was that I didn't have "a dog in the fight." I simply didn't understand the issue. But I did know my needs, and I was doing all I could for my family.

I worked late into Saturday morning. I was getting tired, and it was hard to stay awake. I asked, "How do I get out of here—escape, if you please—safely?"

They worked it all out. The workers outside were the leanest between three and four, and at that time, the managers would distract them.

I got paid what seemed like a ton of money—cash in pocket, and then we planned and executed my escape. "OK, thanks," I said. Let's do it!

I made it past the guys standing in the line, but I got followed by a man in a pickup truck. Off we went through crazy town streets. But I didn't head home yet. I had to lose this guy first. For over a half hour, we were in a serious car chase. He was out to get me. I had to thank my old friend Jim Lamping, who taught me how to really drive a car. Even in my old Chrysler wagon, I was able to ditch that guy and his big truck. And oh, did I mention his shotgun rack?

I don't quite remember how many hours I worked straight, but it was about thirty-six, and they had paid more than I had expected. I even had a little to pay toward college in February. I was still behind, but the important point here: the Lord had provided.

Shortly after that, I finally got a job, as a dishwasher of all things. It was so humbling, but I knew restaurant work well, from back in the days of living in the tree, and I just figured that in time I would work my way up. It was a short-term job, but it was a regular income, and I needed it badly.

Just like I had hoped, one thing, one person, one situation happened. Almost weekly, I was asked, "Hey, Willis, can you pick up a couple more hours next week?" Sure. "Hey, Willis, do you know how to do this or that?" Sure. And then, finally, the cook didn't show up. *Wowzers.*

I was back in the kitchen, and the manager came to see me. We hadn't talked much, but he was in need and had a hunch. "Willis, you seem to know your way around the kitchen, I bet you've cooked in the past...haven't you?"

"Well yes, I have."

"Do you want to try it out tonight?"

"Sure, but do I get any training or help?"

"Not really, but we're shorthanded tonight. We can use you! Do you want to give it a try?"

I asked, "For regular cook's pay, right?"

He said, "Of course," and away we went.

The first thing I did was call all the servers (waitresses back then). "OK, here's the deal. We all fall or rise to the occasion tonight together. I'm going to give you my best shot, but I need your help. You've got the freedom to tell me everything about the plate and the order, as we all know I haven't done any cooking here. But I have cooked elsewhere, and again, together we can do this."

They nervously agreed. Ha! Nobody had a choice. They thought their tips for the night would be trashed. The restaurant wasn't in a great position. It had been several years since I had cooked, and now I was going cold turkey! I had become familiar with the kitchen, and that helped. I had talked to the manager and suggested a few items be taken off the menu for a few nights, and he agreed. So things were streamlined.

The night began fast—luckily not hard, but fast. At least it seemed that way at first. I was cooking and digging out food and hollering to the women, "Tell me more. What's this plate look like? How's it going? What do you need?" I continued to encourage them to overcommunicate. Here's a teaching moment about restaurants: everything depends on the relationships between the server and the cook—everything! If that's fine, everything works so much easier. I knew that was my number-one goal—communicating with them well. The food is a close second, so I had to try hard to show that to them.

At the end of the evening, almost everything had gone OK, acceptable, or repaired. I was exhausted at every level. The manager even got someone to show me how to clean up the cooking area—thankfully. Because that night I became the night cook. It was exciting really, a big step from dishwasher, and a big pay raise. But it came with more mental attention. I couldn't be brain-dead doing my job, and there was no casual studying on the side.

Over the months, I learned to cook everything to the specs. I got along with most of the servers as well as a cook can. It was pretty good. Some of them were just grouchy people or had bad issues in life and with cooks before and were always defensive. But I found ways to sweeten them up. My personality was changing, I was trying to solve conflict with kindness, not more conflict, and it was powerful and enjoyable. *It worked.* It became quite a routine for everyone—a smooth-running machine. And with me, there was always some humor, fun, and tricks to keep it light and fun.

I occasionally mentioned to my boss that summer was coming, and I'd be taking that week off to go back to Florida. My wife and I had family who wanted to see us, especially our new son Joshua, who had been born during all of this. I also had a big issue with my speech class. Right at the end of the semester, my professor did not like my final and was going to fail me. It's another side story we'll skip, but the result was that I took a summer class to make up for the lost credit. Taking that class extended my time at work, and I guess the restaurant just hoped that I wouldn't take off, even though I told them I had to go.

So the day we had to leave was approaching, and I asked about the dates for my vacation. I didn't get anywhere. Finally, I went into the manager's office and asked what was up. He looked at me sternly and told me I couldn't take the week off. I said, "I've told you this since I first got my job here and reminded you when I got promoted. You always acknowledged me, and now you're saying I can't. But you know I have to go." I simply left his office and worked my shift.

I had a *huge* decision to make. Despite all the effort to get the job, God was still impressing on my heart to take a week off to go see our families and preach at our home church that Sunday night. I went to the manager's office two days later and told him I had to go. He said, "You can't."

"Then I have to quit," I said, and I walked out. It was the strangest thing that had ever happened to me at that time. Something was leading me, and it wasn't me.

As I walked out, all I could think about was what was God up to? Everything I'd worked for was gone. What did He have planned for Florida?

The next day we began the long twenty-five-hour drive home with our baby, Joshua. The family situation was tenuous at best. The church expectations were high and excited, and I was unsure what would happen there. It was very intimidating. Do you remember my speech class way back in the tenth grade when I stood up in front of the class and froze, never saying a word? I became the wrestling manager to get a C. Now in Bible college or "preacher school," I had just failed my first speech class. I was scared to death! Nevertheless, I knew God was leading me.

In those days, I argued with God a lot. I didn't think this was funny at all. "Look, God, I have many things I can do, but you are picking the two weakest things in my life to focus on, and I told you I can't do them. And when I do, I do them very poorly. Surely, God, you can find something else for me to do. Really, God?"

His message, thoughts, impressions, calling, whatever you want to call it, never changed or wavered. They stayed crystal clear.

I had surrendered my life to him, and I meant it. I just didn't dream it would be this. So we went back home to St. Pete. I quietly prayed and pleaded, "God, don't leave me now!"

We got back home and saw all the families, and of course, Joshua was a big hit. He was clearly the showcase and helped with many family challenges. Sunday evening came, and it was time for me to preach. The pastor was an awesome preacher of God. He preached for forty-five minutes, throwing out Bible verses like candy at the parade. It was an intimidating act to follow. Plus, a lot of my family was there—my grandmother, my dad and his wife, my aunt, two sisters, and several others. It was a big attendance for Sunday night.

I had my message ready, and I began to preach. I thought I was "waxing eloquent," but when I looked down to see how long I had preached for, it had only been eighteen minutes, and I was finished. I had nothing else to say.

The pastor and I passed each other on the podium. His black hair, black eyebrows, and black eyes were so intimidating, and he was clearly disappointed.

But he gave a proper conclusion to the thoughts of the matter and gave an invitation for salvation. The first one down the aisle was my dad. He was followed by my grandmother, my aunt Patricia, my dad's wife, my sister Karen, and several others. After the service, the pastor and I crossed each other on the podium again, and I had a huge spring in my step a grin on my face and a great countenance of victory. As he stared at me, I laughed and said, "I got the spirit!" Oh yes, there was room for improvement. There still is.

I saw the Holy Spirit touch so many in my family's lives where they too could experience the wonderful redemption of our Lord and Savior. I could only think of one thing: "Worthy is the Lamb of God." At that moment, I realized what it's like to be spirit filled. God showed up. He didn't leave me. He overcame me. What would have happened if I had chosen not to follow the Holy Spirit in my life?

A few days later, we drove back to the college campus. I hadn't even unloaded the car yet, and Larry, an upperclassman, came running over. He said, "Jim, you need to go to the Pepsi plant right now and apply for the job on the production line."

I got back in the car and did just that. I don't know how to explain it. I can't tell you how many people were in line to get that job because it was the best job in town for a college student. I got the job and kept it for the next three years.

So not following reason or logic but following the filling and leadership of the Holy Spirit may not be rational or realistic or popular, but it is rewarding. God became the worthy Lamb to be worshipped and praised. Glory to His name. The security of God continually outweighs the insecurity of the world and my personal worries. Quitting that job was a big step. But wait, there's a second part to the story. I don't want it to sound too easy because it wasn't. I was used to doing things on my own.

By the way, the church and our families raised and gave me enough money toward our ministry that it paid off my whole first year of college expenses. You should've seen that bookkeeper's eyes when I gave her all that money. Paid in full! Even she saw God was working. And I got my report cards too.

THE TRUTH TO BE LEARNED—SECURITY

Just saying that makes no sense at all. Do you remember my story? I knew God wanted me to go back to my home church to do the scariest thing I had ever done, preach. And to do it in front of many friends and lots of family and, of course, watched and observed by my pastor. Intimidating, yes. I was scared to death, yes. Secure? Are you kidding me? Yet a still, small voice inside knew I was doing the right thing. And I had to quit my job that took me all year to get. It just didn't make any sense at all, and I definitely didn't have security...yet.

I hope I'll be able to convey some of the amazing inner workings of my life during those ten hot days in July. You already know how it worked out—amazing beyond "dreams come true." I truly wanted to follow God all the way in my life. That's why I was in Bible college in the first place. By the way, I was the first one in my family to go to college. (All my kids got at least their bachelor's degrees.)

I'm just saying that God can do things you can only dream about. But "if" you let Him be in control of your life, it's like having turbo thrusters that don't run out! This was an all-in God saying He wanted control—total control—of my life, my job, my family, my spiritual growth. It's like surrendering, but more. It's like separation, but more. Because what comes with it is the wow, why, what, when, where, and who of your Christian walk and life.

You are now in the game! Up to this point, you have hopefully been a fan, maybe even a promoter or a groupie. Maybe you were trying out for the team and have been at several practices. But after that moment, you know you're in the game. When you realize that He's talking to you and you hear him saying, "Let me be in control of your life." Your heart starts pounding, and the thoughts are just flying all over the place. It's put up or shut up time, and you know it—and you will. The time when you are most insecure you have ever been, you're just inches, one step, away from being the most secure you have ever been in your life. And it won't go away. Yes, it's crazy. Yes, it's countercultural. No, most Christians haven't done it.

Tozer says, "Religious content is the enemy of the spiritual life always." Yes, it takes trust. That's faith. Yes, it takes courage! But when I was able to look back and review those ten days, God was there, literally. He loves me, and He knows what I really want. He does know what I need. He does care about me intimately, and not just in general. He cares about me, my family, my ministry, my fear, dreams, and success. My God, my Deliverer, my Redeemer, the worthy Lamb of God who wanted to do and would do just for me. That's security!

THE TEXT EMPHASIZED
WHAT HINDERS A BELIEVER FROM BEING
FILLED WITH THE HOLY SPIRIT?

1. Lack of Knowledge (2 Pet. 1:3, 4)
   "As His divine power has given to us all things that pertain to life and godliness, through the knowledge of Him who called us by glory and virtue, by which have been given to us exceedingly great and precious promises, that through these you may be partakers of the divine nature, having escaped the corruption that is in the world through lust."
2. Lack of Desire (John 7:37–39)
   "On the last day, that great day of the feast, Jesus stood and cried out, saying, "If anyone thirsts, let him come to Me and drink. He who believes in Me, as the Scripture has said, out of his heart

will flow rivers of living water." But this He spoke concerning the Spirit, whom those believing in Him would receive; for the Holy Spirit was not yet given, because Jesus was not yet glorified."

3. Lack of Faith (Eph. 5:18)
"And do not be drunk with wine, in which is dissipation; but be filled with the Spirit." Simply put, what will you "Fill yourself up" with...drinks and the world or the Holy Spirit? That's why we are calling it "growing in Christ." When are you going to trust God enough to let him be in control of all your life?

4. Lack of Awareness (Gal. 5:16, 17)
This translation of Galations 5:16, 17 is from Kenneth S. Wuest's book, *Wuest Word Studies,* Volume III. "I say then: Walk in the Spirit, and you shall not fulfill the lust of the flesh. For the flesh lusts against the Spirit, and the Spirit against the flesh; and these are contrary to one another, so that you do not do the things that you wish."

I would like to add Wuest's tremendous summary of the verse. He says, "Be constantly conducting yourselves within the sphere of the Spirit." That is, determine every thought, word, and deed by the leading of the Spirit through the Word, and think every thought, speak every word, and to do every deed in the attitude of entire dependence upon the Holy Spirit's empowering energy, "Bringing into captivity every thought to be obedient of Christ" (2 Cor. 10:5).

Wowzers, people...I suggest reading that several more times. It is *awesome.*

Also, read the great passages from Acts 1:18, John 14:16, 17, Romans 7:15–25, and John 4:23, 24.

THE TITLE...THE NAME OF GOD - WORTHY LAMB; REDEEMER

There are over 120 names for God. They are an amazing study, devotion, or just a great way to start prayer. I truly love to go through the list and meditate on one or two. What an all-encompassing God we have. I have second-guessed myself several times on my choice in this section, worthy Lamb—Redeemer.

I mean the lamb has such significance in Jewish and Christian worship and sacrifice. Even John the Baptist said, "Behold! The Lamb of God who takes away the sin of the world!" (John 1:29). The lamb is characterized as being meek and gentle (Matt. 11:28–30), and so is Jesus. But what possible connection does this have to the filling of the Holy Spirit and Redeemer? Redeemer is a huge word. It is in Genesis and all the way through to Revelation, and why do I connect here with the Holy Spirit?

I have reflected several times about this, and it always goes back to my feeling of worthiness to be captured by God Himself and Him wanting to work in and through me. Am I worth it? No, but because of the lamb of God, I am worthy! And because of His redemption of me, I have been made worthy to participate in this amazing relationship of being filled by part of the Trinity, the Holy Spirit Himself. I'm just saying cool, wowzers, amazing. This all brought me to a place in Revelations 5:9–14:

And they sang a new song, saying: "You are worthy to take the scroll, And to open its seals; For You were slain, And have redeemed us to God by Your blood Out of every tribe and tongue and people and nation, And have made us kings and priests to our God; And we shall reign on the earth." Then I looked, and I heard the voice of many angels around the throne, the living creatures, and the elders; and the number of them was ten thousand times ten thousand, and thousands of thousands, saying with a loud voice: "Worthy is the Lamb who was slain To receive power and riches and wisdom, And strength and honor and glory and blessing!" And every creature which is in heaven and on the earth and under the earth and such as are in the sea, and all that are in them, I heard saying: "Blessing and honor and glory and power Be to Him who sits on the

throne, And to the Lamb, forever and ever!" Then the four living creatures said, "Amen!" And the twenty-four elders fell down and worshiped
Him who lives forever and ever.

Simply put, I am so thankful to be a part of one who is singing this "new
song." And I was simply overwhelmed that if God did all this for me, I should
gratefully let Him do with my life as He wishes. I am so excited about this
growth step, this relationship with my worthy Lamb—Redeemer that I am
encouraging you to take that step, be transformed and renewed, grow in grace,
and be "in Christ" and a follower of "the way."

Listen to the still, small voice. Sometimes it gets louder. Become an obedient child of God, allowing Him, your heavenly Father, control all of your life,
being filled, empowered, and directed by the Holy Spirit. Live constantly for
Him in every word, deed, and thought. Could this be a Defining Moment in
your life that might well be a Divine Appointment? Has something like this
ever happened to you? If so, write it out. If not, why not now?

"Saying with a loud voice: 'Worthy is the Lamb who was slain To receive
power and riches and wisdom, And strength and honor and glory and blessing!'" (Rev. 5:12).

Think about it…He wants to give all of this to you and me right now, all
day, all night, all of our lives.

THEOLOGICAL TEACHING OF…BEING FILLED WITH THE HOLY SPIRIT

(Much of the introduction material is taken from the
Campus Crusade for Christ booklet, *The
Christian and the Holy Spirit.*)

Who is the Holy Spirit, and what is His role in our lives?

The Holy Spirit is God, the third person of the Trinity. He is equal in every way with the Father and the Son. He came to bear witness to the Lord Jesus Christ and glorify Him (John 16:13, 14). When Jesus ascended into heaven, He sent the Holy Spirit to be the Comforter or Helper. The Greek word for "comforter" means "one called along beside" the believer as a companion and friend, and also one who energizes, strengthens, and empowers the believer in Christ.

At the time of our spiritual birth, the Holy Spirit:

- *Regenerates* us (John 3:5–6)
- Comes to *dwell* within us (1 Cor. 3:16)
- *Seals* us in Christ (Eph. 4:30)
- *Baptizes* us into the body of Christ (1 Cor. 12:13)
- *Fills* and *empowers* us for service (Acts 1:8, Eph. 5:18)

What is the Spirit-filled life? The Spirit-filled life is the Christ-filled life. In a very real sense, Christians give up their lives, spiritual impotence, defeat, and fruitlessness for the power and victory of Jesus Christ. According to Ephesians 5:18, it is living "under the influence" or control (continuously" loving) of the Holy Spirit. To be filled with the Spirit, however, does not mean that we receive more of the Holy Spirit but that we give Him more of ourselves. Every biblical reference to the filling of the Holy Spirit in both the Old Testament and the New Testament relates to power for service and witness.

What is the status of and potential for every believer? Dr. Billy Graham has said that according to his research, at least 90 percent of all Christians in America are living defeated lives (90 percent stand). Why are so many Christians living in defeat? They are not living in God's power. In other words, they are not filled with the Holy Spirit. Basically, the problem involves the will. There is not a willingness to submit to the Lordship of Jesus Christ. The result is that many Christians learn to "fake it," but inside they are miserable because there is no one more miserable than a Christian out of fellowship with Christ.

Through the centuries, the great majority of followers of Christ were just ordinary Christians. Nothing spectacular ever happened to them or through them. Then, as happened to Peter and his disciples, they were filled with the Holy Spirit, and their lives were changed. They were no longer average. They became men and women of God, instruments of power. They were the ones who "turned the world upside down."

Wouldn't *you* like to become "one of them" who "turned the world upside down"? It is at your fingertips. It is God's desire for you. But unlike several other growth steps, with this one you *must* be totally surrendered to God. If you are desperate for His power, His comfort, His will in your life, you will want to do this. Yes, it is a big step of faith. Yes, it begins with a lot of insecurity (just like me quitting my job made no worldly sense). But, in the end, you will have great comfort, total security, and the thrill of a lifetime walking with God—and knowing it.

Come on; take the jump! It is when, as Pastor Mike Kahn says, "Ordinary men and women, who are filled with an extraordinary God…become extraordinary men and women." Let's see what it's all about.

THE HOLY SPIRIT AND THE BELIEVER

The disciples were to tarry in Jerusalem waiting for Pentecost (Luke 24:29). Acts 2:4 was the fulfillment of this promise when the Spirit came to abide. Every believer has the Holy Spirit, but the Spirit does not control each believer. Believer still have stubborn rebellious will. They may pray or not, give or not, witness or not, surrender or not. They may obey or resist and grieve the Spirit. The crowning act of faith is for believers to relinquish their lives to the Spirit. This is not necessary for salvation, but it is necessary to be Spirit filled. The infilling is received when believers consciously recognize the Holy Spirit as being in full control of their lives, completely governing every detail of life.

FILLING IS A COMMAND TO BE OBEYED

Is this wonderful experience a luxury for only a few people like the apostles and Stephen? It ought to be the experience of every believer. Ephesians 5:18 is not an optional command. Saintly S. D. Gordon in *The Ministry of the Spirit* says to be "God-intoxicated men." The picture in Ephesians 5:18 is a contrast between a man under the influence, completely directed by another power, either wine (earthly) or the Spirit (heavenly).

Egypt always has the Nile, but Egypt waits each year for its overflow. Having the Nile is one thing but having the overflowing Nile is quite another. When the Nile overflows, Egypt is refreshed. Let us know the overflowing Spirit (John 7:38, 39). The original Greek language is in the imperative progressive—keep on being filled. Let the filling be constant and continuous. The apostle Peter was filled with the Spirit in Acts 2:4 and again in Acts 4:8 and again in Acts 4:31. Each day needs its own new fullness.

EVERYONE NEEDS THE FILLING OF THE SPIRIT

Every believer in Jesus Christ needs the filling of the Holy Spirit. The filling is for the apostles, preachers, fathers, mothers, teens, young people, and children. We each need it for our own benefit to be the best possible Christian. Without it, we cannot attain to the Lord's will for us regarding character and service. The filling of the Spirit is an individual blessing. People are saved and filled individually. The filling must be individually received. I must personally do business with God. The Spirit cannot illuminate our minds, warm our affections, purge our consciences, or energize our wills until we surrender to Him and keep surrendered.

THE CHURCH NEEDS EVERY MEMBER TO BE SPIRIT FILLED

Sometimes unwise, extravagant, and fanatical things are done in the name of the filling of the Holy Spirit. Because of this, many believers shun the filling.

Some say that the ability to speak in tongues is the proof of the Spirit filling. The Bible says that tongues are a sign to the unbelievers of the reality of the Gospel to change lives (1 Cor. 14:22). The church needs Spirit-filled members. If the filling is lacking, the church is plagued with disorders, dissensions, strife, backbiting, jealousy, and scandal. Let every member of the church be Spirit filled, the pastor, elders, deacons, Sunday-school teachers, singers, choir members, and ordinary church members.

THE WORLD EXPECTS BELIEVERS TO BE SPIRIT FILLED

Our Christian walk is twofold: (1) Godward and (2) outward to fellowmen. The world expects every Christian to be almost perfect. To live up to the world's imaginary standard, every believer desperately needs the Spirit filling. We cannot be effective witnesses if we are not Spirit filled. To do the work of the Lord in the energy of the flesh can only lead to disappointment and failure. Spirit-filled believers, living the crucified life in relation to the world, are effective means in the Lord's hands to convict and convince sinners.

CONDITIONS OF FILLING BY THE HOLY SPIRIT

A. **Forgiveness**. "Repent, and let every one of you be baptized in the name of Jesus Christ for the remission of sins; and you shall receive the gift of the Holy Spirit" (Acts 2:38)

B. **Sonship**. "And because you are sons, God has sent forth the Spirit of His Son into your hearts, crying out, "Abba, Father!" (Gal. 4:6).

C. **Desire**. "If, any man thirst..." (John 7:37–39, also Isa. 44:3).

D. **Faith**. "The Spirit given to those who believe" (John 7:39, also (Gal. 3:13, 14).

E. **Obedience**. "He gives the Holy Ghost to those who obey Him" (Acts 5:32).

F. **Waiting.** "Wait for the promise of the Father" (Luke 24:49, Acts 1:4). Be unhurried.

G. **Prayer.** "The Holy Spirit given to those who ask Him" (Luke 11:13, also, Act 4:31).

H. **Appropriate the fact.** "Ask and receive" (John 1:12). "Take the gift of the filling and live, and act as if the transaction were real and genuine" (Luke 11: 9, 10).

The secret to being filled with the Holy Spirit is surrender, surrendering our wills, bodies, possessions, and every aspect of our lives to His control.

RESULTS OF BEING SPIRIT FILLED

A. Power to witness is one mighty manifestation of a Spirit-filled saint (Acts 1:8).

B. Power to live victorious Christian life (Acts 20:22–24, Paul speaking to Ephesians).

C. Glory will certainly accrue to the Lord (John 16:14, the Spirit's basic ministry).

D. The infilling of the Spirit is the indispensable qualification for all holy living.

E. The Holy Spirit quickens the intellect, affections, conscience, will, and personality.

F. The filling is the secret of abiding, obeying, and God-honoring trust in the Word.

CONCLUSION

We are not reservoirs but channels. We must overflow. Blessings must pour out. Conversion first, and then filling and overflowing. This is beautifully pictured in the Bible pictures of the working of the Holy Spirit.

1. An overflowing spring (John 4:14)
2. Overflowing fountain (John 7:37–39)
3. An abundance of sap in the tree (Rom. 8:11)
4. As overflowing waters (Eph. 5:18). Remember that the filling is not a once-for-all experience. It must be repeated daily.

TESTING AND TRIALS IF YOU CHOOSE NOT TO LIVE FILLED BY HOLY SPIRIT

This list could be quite long, which should indicate the extreme importance of this step of growth. It is, without a doubt, the most powerful life-changing experience apart from salvation. Without the filling of the Holy Spirit and His control in your life, you will probably feel, or be frustrated by several things:

1. The lack of God's power in your life
2. The lack of God's control in your life
3. The lack of God's direction in your life
4. The lack of confidence in God in your life
5. The lack of comfort in your life
6. The lack of belonging to God's family
7. The lack of "feeling His presence"
8. The lack of miracles in your life
9. The lack of excitement in your life

And, just to name a few, these following things will be predominant in your life instead of the Holy Spirit:

1. You will lack knowledge of what God wants.
2. You will be full of pride in yourself.
3. You will be fearful of men or women.
4. You will be haunted frequently by your secret sins.

5. You will be "on the fence," guilty of being worldly.
6. You'll be frustrated that you don't have enough faith in God.
7. You won't experience the thrill, joy, and power of being empowered by the Holy Spirit.

THE TRIBUTE SONG

"Spirit of the Living God"
Daniel Iverson

Spirit of the living God, fall afresh on me.
Spirit of the living God, fall afresh on me.
Melt me, mold me, fill me, use me,
Spirit of the living God, fall afresh on me.
Spirit of the living God, fall afresh on us.
Spirit of the living God, fall afresh on us.
Melt us, mold us, fill us, use us,
Spirit of the living God, fall afresh on us.

9

New Battles – New Enemies!

I HAD BEEN saved for six years and had successfully graduated with a four-year bachelor's in theology degree. Though 470 students started our freshman year, only 174 graduated. It was in 1981. For whatever reason, very few of us got a job that year, but thankfully, I was one of five. It happened to be back in Florida on the southeast coast. I had met with the pastor several times when he had come up to college and interviewed several people. We seemed to hit it off, and we had both clearly identified our ministry goals—which were many! We were both extremely excited and anxious.

I was to be the associate pastor, youth pastor, and acting principal of a Christian school. Looking back, wasn't that just a bit much to ask a new guy to do? Maybe it was because I was new, but all the ministries I was involved in were growing. Teenagers were excited, and the school and the teachers were doing great and were all pleased. The services on Wednesday night, when I was teaching, had grown phenomenally. Maybe it was just to hear the new guy, but I was excited.

Then completely unexpectedly, unseen, and unanticipated, I was blind-sided by jealousy—in the ministry, no less. They hadn't taught us how to deal with that in Bible college. The whole point of me coming down was to support the pastor and help grow the church. I felt extremely blessed and was dedicated to doing that. The first battle that rose in my ministry was a battle of the flesh—jealousy. We had several awkward conversations where the pastor was clearly uncomfortable and continued to make things harder on me.

And then there was the battle of Satan. I call this the sin of the preacher's son. One of the teens in the youth department was the pastor's oldest son. He was a handful, and one fateful afternoon I caught him with a bag of pot, smoking a joint behind the church school. They didn't teach me how to deal with that in college either.

After several hours of prayer, I decided to call the pastor of my home church in St Pete, Florida. He assured me and counseled me that I *must* tell the pastor, this kid's father. I predicted that it wouldn't go well, but he continued to encourage me to do what was right. I called my pastor—the father of this boy—asking if I could see him right away. We met at his house, and I brought the evidence, and the son confessed. I learned that when you stack humiliation on top of jealousy, you will find rage—a very defensive characteristic. In our conversation that evening, the pastor basically told me to pack my bags and leave, even though the ministry was thriving and growing. My dreams were being crushed and cut off.

What was particularly fascinating and timely was that I had been going through the book of Ephesians on the Wednesday-night Bible study. We had covered the wealth and the walk and were in discussion on the warfare the very week that this all came to a head—the thirteenth week of study. (Talk about God putting a plan together!) It was during this time that I had learned to put on the full armor of God, not just for a happy day, not just for a day of opportunity but for battle. As servants/soldiers, God wants us to serve Him in good times and bad, whether we are satisfied and successful or suffering. We are to always put on the full armor of God with not just obedience but joy in our hearts and a life that will glorify Him. It is this armor that we put on and take with us that will always give us victory.

Here is the story, the moment, the appointment, the time in my life when I *knew* God was talking to me about my next growth step. All of us have been in some type of service for the Lord. Sometimes we have been told to do something because leadership thinks that we are available or capable. Sometimes we get involved in the project because it is satisfying and something we like to do. Other times, I've seen people involved in ministry and church because it's opportunistic or makes them look successful.

But we're talking about a different level of servanthood. That's why we are using this particular story to identify a Defining Moment in my life and ministry that was very much a Divine Appointment. The point is that God wants us to serve Him in all circumstances—not just through obedience but with love and joy in our hearts even when it involves suffering.

THE TRUTH LEARNED SUFFERING AND AFFLICTIONS

If you remember, all my other growth steps were changes and challenges and took courage, but they weren't crushing or hurtful. This one was. This one hurt a lot. As you know, I grew up fighting regularly—I'm talking about physical fighting. It was for many different reasons: to defend myself from my older sister, to resist being bullied, or because I had a chip on my shoulder, was involved in a gang war, and sometimes just because I wanted to. It's what I did. It was the only way I knew how to fix a conflict. (Just writing that down really hurts all by itself.)

The point is that I knew pain physically, but mental pain was the worst. I got used to it (oh my, that too is an awful place to be). I had learned that in these circumstances, if I give into the pain, I would experience a lot more of it. So I disciplined myself to think that pain was not weakness, and I retaliated with a vengeance and overcame that moment many times, simply for survival. I remember frequently telling my two sons (they are awesome grown men now) that fighting hurts. Even when you win, it often still hurts. Find another way to solve problems. Figure it out; you're smart enough. And Lord knows my sons were "clever" enough to get into or out of anything they did.

After becoming a Christian and growing quickly in His grace, I learned and experienced His love, peace, and joy. I worked a lot in the church even early on. There are a bunch of unusual people who go to church. Many of them are quite "different." Do we all think that, or is it just me? I met and loved many different kinds of people, and I realized that God loved them too. Go figure. So I had left the fighting world of the flesh, thankfully, and I was cruising in this work for Christ. The conflicts during my time of soul winning were minor, particularly in comparison to my past.

So when the pastor, the one who had trusted me in his church pulpit, and then fired me because I caught his son smoking pot, completely turned on me in, I was blindsided. In the old days, I became aware of my surrounding and people's movements so I could protect myself. Did I let my guard down? Was I supposed to have my guard up? What happened? Why? The "spiritual wind" was knocked right out of me. *Wowzers.*

It's interesting how we know "stuff," but we don't know "stuff." Let me explain. I knew I was a servant of God. That was all I wanted to do and be. I also knew I was in God's army. But I obviously didn't know what that really entailed until then. In the days following, I began to understand that in service for God, there *is* going to be some suffering, some afflictions, and maybe even some persecution, and that they should be expected. What a surprise that was. But look at the scriptures. They are very clear about it.

By the way, I was able to come to the realization of this truth by looking hard at the Bible and what it says. My whole purpose for writing this book is to tell you that God does speak to us when we read, study, and meditate on His word *and* through the Holy Spirit. Have you heard Him? Did you listen? And did you obey him and therefore are "growing in Christ"? What is your story?

So the truth learned was *suffering and afflictions.* There are lots of similar words in the Bible that I share in this concept and principle. They are bear, endure hardship, anguish, distress, persecution, strained, pressed, thronged, suffering, tribulation, troubles, and violence, just to mention a few. Here is a short list of verses that share these words and concepts: 2 Corinthians 11:19, Hebrews 13:22, 1 Thessalonians 2:2, Romans 8:17, Hebrews 11:25, 1 Peter 5:9, 2 Peter 2:13, 1 Corinthians 9:12, 2 Timothy 2:12, Philippians 4:12, 2 Timothy 3:11, Hebrews 10:32.

Suffering—afflicted; in pain
Need prayer in…James 5:13

Suffering for Christ
Necessary in Christian living…1 Corinthians 12:26; Philippians 1:29
Blessed in privilege…Acts of the Apostles 5:41
Never in vain…Galatians 3:4
After Christ's example…Philippians 3:10; 1 Peter 2:20, 21
Of short duration…1 Peter 5:10
Not comparable to heaven's glory…Romans 8:18; 1 Peter 4:13

Sufferings of Christ
A. *Features concerning:*
    Predicted…1 Peter 1:11
    Announced…Mark 9:12
    Explained…Luke 24:26, 46
    Fulfilled…Acts of the Apostles 3:18
    Witnessed…1 Peter 5:1
    Proclaimed…Acts of the Apostles 17:2, 3
B. *Benefits of and to Christ*
    Preparation for priesthood…Hebrews 2:17, 18
    Learned obedience…Hebrews 5:8
    Way to glory…Hebrews 2:9, 10

C. *Benefits of and to Christians:*
Brought to God...1 Peter 3:18
Our sins atoned...Hebrews 9:26–28
Example...1 Peter 2:21–23
Fellowship...Philippians 3:10
Consolation...2 Corinthians 1:5–7

THE TEXT EMPHASIZED
EPHESIANS 2:10 AND EPHESIANS 6:10–18

"For we are His workmanship, created in Christ Jesus for good works, which God prepared beforehand that we should walk in them" (Eph. 2:10).

And really, we can't even start to share what this verse *does* and *does not* mean until we review verses 8 and 9. Verse 8 states, "For by grace you have been saved through faith, and that not of yourselves; it is the gift of God." Verse 9 states, "Not of works, lest anyone should boast."

These are popular and powerful verses that are clear about how we can get saved. They simply say that you didn't do it, and you can't do enough to get it; you don't have the wherewithal to do it or get it. It's not about you. God has done it all for you. God has provided everything for us. It's all simply a gift from God because He chooses to be very gracious to us, and we have nothing that we can take credit for. Period.

Yeah, yeah, I know that's tough on our personal accomplishment area. It's brutal on our self-pride area too, isn't it? We always like to think and say that we had a part in everything, but God is making it perfectly clear. You did nothing to get this wonderful free gift of God's grace and all that comes with it.

Let me share one more biblical principle. You don't even deserve it because you were full of so much sin that you are offensive to God's holiness.

This is why He had to do something/everything to clean us up! And that takes a lot of love. And we are thankful that God is love and that He loves us. Praise the Lord, people.

So when we get to verse 10, "Created in Christ Jesus unto good works," guess what? They are not works and things that we necessarily know how to do already. They are "his workmanship." God gave us a new life of eternity, and He wants to fashion us into His new spiritual handiwork. With this new life in Christ comes new spiritual responsibilities that God Himself has placed within us, and which can only be accomplished through Christ Jesus. It's still all about him.

In my life, I see it quite clearly. I was a poor student and a poor reader, and I was *never* a public speaker. It was a challenging, courageous, five-year time span in my life. But God transformed me in every way possible yet kept me, my personality that He had created, intact. Amazing! So it is easy for me to give God all the glory for what has happened in my life because it is so completely obvious. I don't say that with boasting. It's done with clear gratefulness that He thought of me and uses me to this day. Praise God. Amen.

You see:

God had this "view" of my life work.
God had the "object" of my life work in Him.
God has "ordained them" beforehand in my life.
God has us "walking through" these plans even before we are saved.
Think about that one for a while.

All other religions are set up by good works. That means that you get nothing until you do all their good works. Then you can have all this "good stuff."

But God and Christianity don't do it that way. First, at our salvation, God gives us everything spiritually speaking. Then He says, "OK, you're saved now. Have no fear or worries about your future. I've got you; you are mine. I love you, and I will keep you and never ever leave you. Now we have some work to do—together. I need you to do this for my kingdom because there are still many, many more of my children lost out there, and we must find them. But don't worry. I've got this. You're going to be doing some different things you didn't know you could do, but you can because I have designed you for the job/opportunity by gifting this ability to you as well. OK. Let's get to work in Christ Jesus."

Expositors says, "We are God's spiritual handiwork in the sense that we were created by Him, made a new spiritual creature by Him and His grace made us Christians."

Vincent says, "God prearranged a sphere of moral action for us to walk in. Not only are works the necessary outcome of faith, but the character and direction of the works are made by God."

Expositors comments, "His final object was to make good works the very element of our life, the domain in which our actions should move. *Our Christian walk should mirror His handiwork.*"

Ephesians 6:10–18 is covered in our theological teaching, but I want to simply make a clear application that seems to be so obviously ignored, forgotten, and disobeyed, or people are simply not aware of it.

We are in spiritual warfare.

We really do have spiritual enemies.

They really do want to harm us any way they can.

We really do have to fight—like it or not. When you got "saved," you left the devil's army and moved on to God's army, and Satan is *not happy.* He never really is anyway. He and his army are mean, deceptive liars who only want to demean us and destroy our testimony of the wonderful work that Jesus Christ has done for us.

Listen. We are not in Beulah Land…yet.
We are not in the Promised Land…yet.
We are not in heaven…yet.

When you and I got saved by God's saving grace, we were immediately enlisted into the army of God. And let me tell you, it is for life or death—eternity. God, the church, and the lost need you more than ever to "armor up." Get in the game/battle, and fight for the cause of Christ. Deliver the gospel of God's love, grace, and peace. Fascinating, isn't it? Such a contrast. Are you feeling ready for this battle? It's a lot bloodier than you think. Get properly dressed. Armor up!

THE TITLE OF GOD AND ITS APPLICATION

Although I had traveled so far spiritually at this point, from nowhere and nothing to somewhere and something, I was in the ministry—on staff, mind you—and it was working, growing, and exciting.

I had learned and applied the previous Defining Moments that were actually Divine Appointments: *Savior, Lord, Holy One, Redeemer / Worthy Lamb.* I had developed a lot of confidence in what was going on and how to do it. And I was doing it. Awesome. But God knew I needed to grow some more. I needed to *know* this is a battle for the souls of men and women and boys and girls of all ages and lifestyles, and I would need something more than myself as well as more of the power of the Holy Spirit. Because that power would take me to places and into situations where I needed some extra help or protection.

I needed to rely on something besides me and my craftiness. I found out that I needed to rely on something more than others in the ministry or church members. For proper protection in the spiritual battle, I needed to put on the full armor of God (Eph. 6:11).

The enemy, Satan, can and will use anybody and everybody for his wicked purposes. Every day, we need to be not just loaded up with the gospel of Christ but also properly prepared, suited-up, fully armored, and ready for a heated battle.

When we are involved in changing people's lives for Christ, we are not just taking them out of the devil's army, we are also training new believers how to be soldiers in God's army, fighting and resisting spiritual wickedness. Frankly, that makes the devil mad, and yes, it makes God glad. Praise the Lord.

As I looked at the names of God (there are over 120 of them), I saw several that could've worked here: Commander/Leader found in Isaiah 55:4; Mighty God in that popular passage, Isaiah 9:6; or Deliverer found in Romans 11:26. Those are good, but I wanted something more personal. These actual interpretations are for the nation of Israel. Then there's the head of all things: Ephesians 1:22. What a great passage; what a great opening prayer.

By the way, if you remember, I was actually doing a thirteen-week Wednesday-night Bible study, and that is largely part of the problem. The church was having abnormally large crowds on those nights, and this is one of the things that upset the pastor. You'd think he'd be happy or pleased. I never dreamed he'd get flat-out jealous. I was there to help the pastor and the church. He hired me because he saw my passion and abilities. I was doing what he wanted, what the church wanted, and what God called me to do. Perfect...right?

It was not so perfect. The seed of jealousy was growing, and the sins of the preacher's son were the final straw. The pastor was furious, and in the days to follow, I found that I needed the full armor of God (Eph. 6:11), which I was teaching the next Wednesday night. What timing God has. When I taught that night, for the first time in my spiritual life journey, I put on the full armor of God while I was teaching, right in front of the whole church. When it says, "Have your loins girded about in truth, and having on the breastplate of righteousness, and your feet shod with the preparation of the gospel of peace," I claimed them right there on the podium, and I saw many others doing the same. And when the passage transitions to "*taking* the shield of faith wherewith you shall be able to quench all the fiery darts of the wicked and *take* the helmet of salvation, and *take* the sword of the Spirit, which is the word of God," I took them. I picked them up and cleaned them for the battles to come. They have served me well.

As I had to transition out of that church, there were (and for that matter, still are) several questions about why things went the way they did. Many people told me that they were sad to see me go.

I was welcomed back to my home church in St. Pete with open and healing arms. Yes, you and I must wear the full armor of God!

THE THEOLOGICAL TEACHING APPLIED
EPHESIANS 6:10–18

The apostle Paul looked on the centurion soldier who stood by him twenty-four hours a day while he spent his last days in jail. By the way, Paul was in jail only because he was preaching the gospel of Jesus Christ. Many of our persecuted brothers and sisters in the world are being tortured and killed daily for preaching Jesus. You better believe that they learned this spiritual growth step. They have truly given their all for Christ. Jesus is asking you and me to do the same.

Here in America, it's not really that bad, but it's getting worse daily. Our families are struggling, our communities are facing havoc, and our whole country is being pressed beyond measure. Yet Paul delivered the amazing commission while he was in prison "in having done all to stand." It was his final thought, his last request, his conclusion to the riches we have in Christ Jesus. There is not a place to give up, let up, step aside, or stand down for the servant/soldier of Jesus Christ.

Yes, there is the chaos of the world, but we are peace, joy, and life. Yes, there is the persuasiveness of the flesh, but the gospel is real love, forgiveness, and unity. And oh yes, it seems the devil and his team are busier than ever, more powerful, and more influencing, yet we are to be strong. We are to stand because Jesus has called us all in the "great commission to be in the spiritual battle."

In our passage here, we have two major focuses. Verses 10 to 13 describe our enemy and who they are:

[10] "Finally, my brethren, be strong in the Lord and in the power of His might."
[11] "Put on the whole armor of God, that you may be able to stand against the wiles of the devil."
[12] "For we do not wrestle against flesh and blood, but against principalities, against powers, against the rulers of the darkness of this age, against spiritual hosts of wickedness in the heavenly places."
[13] "Therefore take up the whole armor of God, that you may be able to withstand in the evil day, and having done all, to stand."

I'm not really trying to scare you, but maybe I should. Average Christians today seems to be clueless in this battle. They seem to not believe, or maybe they don't realize that Satan and his followers exist, and their only purpose is to destroy us. That's you, Christian. Look at this opening passage. It talks about how we are to be strong. The strength clearly comes from the Lord. That's so we can even have a chance to stand. Do we not see this all around us? We are in spiritual warfare. We are asked to stand against Satan and all his "wiles," his wicked ways, and to resist the devil who attacks us regularly. Amen. Satan is powerful. He does have a lot of principalities and powers against the rulers of the darkness of the world and against spiritual wickedness in high places. Are you really getting this?

If so, let me ask you a question right here now. When something bad happens in your life, why do you blame God? Why God? We supposedly know that God is good. Maybe we are not fully aware of the evil battle we are in and that Satan and his crew are evil and do the bad things to us, not God. He loves us. Again, are we aware of what is going on all around us in the spiritual warfare. Why do we think everything is supposed to be wonderful roses? Even they have thorns! Come on; wake up. You are in the battle, period. Fight like a soldier of God. Let's see how it is completely different than any fight you have ever been in! The *power* is from God, the *protection* is from God, the *provisions* are from God, the *plan* is all God's, and our *perseverance* is all from God.

Let's look at how to fight this battle—and it is a battle for eternity's sake!

Ephesians 6:14–18 is our armor: how to fight
Stand therefore, having girded your waist with truth, having put on the breastplate of righteousness, and having shod your feet with the preparation of the gospel of peace; above all, taking the shield of faith with which you will be able to quench all the fiery darts of the wicked one. And take the helmet of salvation, and the sword of the Spirit, which is the word of God; praying always with all prayer and supplication in the Spirit, being watchful to this end with all perseverance and supplication for all the saints.

YOUR LOINS GIRDED WITH TRUTH (VERSE 14)

This is the region (loins, thighs, hips, lower back) regarded as most crucial to the provision of strength and mobility in combat. The source of strength—a contest of close quarters. "We wrestle." *Implanted truth* is John 14:6: "I am the Way." *Imparted truth:* As wise workers use "the Word of Truth" (2 Cor. 6:7). *Implemented truth:* "With you and in you," the Spirit of the Truth put to work (John 14:17). Truth—a source of liberty. Truth gives freedom (John 8:32). The truth shall set you free. It gives confidence that we know the final battle. Truth—a source of restraint. While truth is our greatest source of liberty, it is at the same time our primary restraining influence.

BREAST PLATE OF RIGHTEOUSNESS (VERSE 14)

This protects all the vital organs of the body from neck to waist. It is a must for hand-to-hand combat. Righteousness of several kinds is found 644 times in scripture. Self-righteousness—worthless (Phil. 3). Imputed righteousness is the foundation of all righteousness (1 Cor. 1:30, Rom. 4:3–5). The position of righteousness—the breastplate—name badge—identifies—apply the character of Christ—heart, lungs (breath), stomach (digestion)—our soul and within. The power of righteousness—new way, new activities, new desires. The path of righteousness "Instruction in righteousness" (1 Tim. 3:16, 17).

YOUR FEET SHOD WITH THE GOSPEL OF PEACE (VERSE 15)

Preparation (feet, ankles, calves)—through habitual readiness—establishes a firm foundation. A powerful message is, "Peace be unto you" (Job 20:21). "Peace I give unto you" (Rom. 1:16). The power of God: "It is the life, death, burial, resurrection (1 Cor. 15:1–4). Purpose: it should direct us to defend the faith (Matt. 28:18) and win the lost in a peaceful way. It is news of divine compassion (love for a guilty, perishing mankind), almighty redemption (our debt is satisfied), glorious resurrection (hope in a new glorified body given), eternal satisfaction (I shall be satisfied when I wake in his likeness) (Ps. 17:15).

SHOES OF THE GOSPEL—ADVERTISEMENT

Timeless design—a universal flavor. No more worrying about changing styles.

Provides incomparable balance and sure footing—no aches or pains.

Soles are made of indestructible material that stands up to the toughest punishment.

The durability is unmatched.

Guaranteed never to wear out—an everlasting shine—at a price that can't be beat!

SHIELD OF FAITH (VERSE 16)

Two kinds of shields (small or large) are to completely protect the soldier. A Shield is provided to protect without much individual maneuvering. Faith, then, is a belief and a trust in God and His Word, the Holy Bible. Faith can be viewed as:

F—Favorable	F—False
A—Actions	E—Evidence
I—Issuing	A—Appearing
T—Through	R—Real
H—Head and heart believe in God	

Faith is, above all, our greatest defense against darts of the devil. Training to use our shields is through reading God's word, the experience of others, and our personal experiences.

HELMET OF SALVATION (VERSE 17)

Purpose: protects the head, the seat of the mind, reason, and intellect. Keeps our thinking straight. Our salvation knows, so it is without doubt and lies and saves us from mental confusion and darkness.

The helmet is used to protect the head. It implies assurance and confidence and is used for identification. Salvation delivers us from the devil's army, is the greatest desire of God, and can be received by trusting in Christ. Salvation to come. "Hope of Salvation," the moment of salvation (Rom. 10:13), the working out of our sin (Heb. 5), and the hope of salvation (1 Thess. 5:8).

This becomes our anchor: Rom. 3:11; Pss. 31:24, 33:18, 39:7, 42:11, 71:5, 146:5; Eph. 2:12; Thess. 4:13–18.

THE SWORD OF THE SPIRIT (VERSE 17)
There are two kinds of swords—the big, slow-moving one and the shorter, quicker one. The primary use was offense. Our sword is inspired by God (2 Tim. 3:16), given through holy men (2 Pet. 1:21), received by only those who believe (Rom. 10:13).

How to fight our three enemies: the world, through faith. "This is the victory, that (faith) overcomes the world" (1 John 5:4). The flesh—we flee. "Flee youthful lust" (1 John 5:4). The devil, we fight. "Submit yourselves to God, Resist the devil and he will flee from you" (James 4:7). It is to be taken (Josh. 1:8; Ps. 119:11, 105, 172); it is very useful (Heb. 4:12)—quick, powerful, sharp.

ASKING OF PRAYER—PRAYING ALWAYS (VERSE 18)
Earnestly, in the Spirit, with perseverance, for boldness to speak the gospel, for comfort of the saints.

Conclusion: Read Ephesians 6:23, 24: "Peace to the brethren, and love with faith, from God the Father and the Lord Jesus Christ. Grace be with all those who love our Lord Jesus Christ in sincerity. Amen."

Review each part of the armor. "Strong in the Lord," having done all to stand, it's up to me to bring glory for thee! Don't just be saved, spirit indwelled, sanctified, and sitting. Be a soldier, standing, strong, sowing, and serving our Savior.

THE TESTING OR TRIAL OF NOT TAKING THIS STEP SERVANT/SOLDIER

I wish I could be much more tactful, kind, sweet, loving, but

1. if you don't get this, you will be spiritually roughed up your whole life;
2. if you don't understand that you are a servant/soldier, you will never be doing what God wants you to do;
3. you may feel a lack of purpose and fulfillment;
4. your experiences of a victorious life will be limited;
5. your core view will be frustrated; it's not about you, It's about what God wants to do with you, your life;
6. Your battles—we all have them—will hurt, and you will experience slow or no healing; and
7. You are likely missing the whole point: people need you to stand up for Christ, hope, love, peace, forgiveness, and joy and tell them the problems with sin and share the love and sacrifice of Jesus to make them whole again. That, my friends, *is the battle*. Getting people saved and born again, taking them out of the devil's destiny, and bringing them to heaven with us.

A PERSONAL PRAYER OF COMMITMENT

Heavenly Father,

I recognize that my primary struggle today will not be against flesh and blood. I know there is more to this life than meets the eye. Help me see people the way You see them and respond accordingly.

Give me the strength to stand my ground against this world. Enable me to recognize its twisted values and perspectives.

Today, I choose to stand firm with the belt of truth buckled around my waist. Bring to my mind what is true when confronted with the lies that permeate this world. As I open Your Word, renew my mind to what is true.

I put on the breastplate of righteousness. Thank you for giving me a righteous standing with You. With Your help, I will live a life that reflects that righteousness. Give me the wisdom to know what's right and the courage to do what's right, even when it is hard.

I put on the shoes of readiness. Where you lead, I will follow. Lead me to those who have not yet accepted your offer of salvation. Give me boldness and sensitivity as I represent You to others.

I take up the shield of faith, which has the power to help me stand against temptation, rejection, doubt, and fear. On the cross, Christ overcame the power of sin on my behalf and proved once and for all that I am fully accepted. His resurrection took away the basis for all my doubt and fear.

I put on the helmet of salvation. My salvation is a reminder of all You have done and will do in me. It is a reminder of who I am and to Whom I belong. You bought me with a price. You must consider me valuable. You have called me Your child. You must consider me lovable.

Lastly, I take up the sword of the Spirit, which is Your Word. Your Word is a lamp to my feet and a light to my path. Through Your Word, bring my ways in line with Your ways and my thoughts in line with Your thoughts.

I ask all of this in the name of Jesus.
Amen

THE TRIBUTE SONG

"Onward, Christian Soldiers"
Sabine Baring-Gould Arthur Sullivan

Onward, Christian soldiers, marching as to war,
With the cross of Jesus going on before.
Christ, the royal Master, leads against the foe;
Forward into battle see His banners go!
At the sign of triumph Satan's host doth flee;
On then, Christian soldiers, on to victory!
Hell's foundations quiver at the shout of praise;
Brothers lift your voices, loud your anthems raise.

Like a mighty army moves the church of God;
Brothers, we are treading where the saints have trod.
We are not divided, all one body we,
One in hope and doctrine, one in charity.

Onward then, ye people, join our happy throng,
Blend with ours your voices in the triumph song.
Glory, laud and honor unto Christ the King,
This through countless ages men and angels sing.

Refrain
Onward, Christian soldiers, marching as to war,
With the cross of Jesus going on before.

10

WHAT'S MINE? WHAT'S HIS?

I CAN'T THINK of any subject that is tougher to talk about than money, particularly in the American church. Over the decades, I have known more people who have been offended when the pastor preached about money. That entire concept, I must confess, completely puzzles me. I guess it's because I keep thinking that people in the church are grown up. But, many are not. The main purpose of writing this book is to let you know the Seven Stepping Stages in the Savior, or our growth steps. This step involves our money. The problem with money and why is it so offensive is because it can't be camouflaged. As a Christian, we all know that our relationship with Jesus Christ comes with financial responsibilities or, as I like to look at them, opportunities. The more we resist God's calling in this area of our life, the more frustration, criticism, and disappointment we will have—more than in any other area of our life.

This story starts eighteen years after I got saved. This clearly identifies that we don't understand all these principles the moment we get saved. It's a concept of being conformed into His image. It's a growth process, and it's being transformed. It's learning how to be *in* Christ Jesus. It's trying to understand "Follow me as I follow Christ," like the apostle Paul said. And these steps aren't accidental. We don't learn these principles through osmosis. There will be a time when God speaks to us, and, if we listen, it could be a Defining Moment in our lives that may well be a Divine Appointment. This is how we need to come to accept, understand, and obey the major growth steps.

I had known for years that I was to give the first 10 percent of my total income to God, and I would give extra at times as we went along. I understood that to mean that the 10 percent was God's, and the 90 percent was mine. For many years, I had been in bi-vocational ministry. That means working at the church and also having a job on the side, plus my family. There were certainly a lot of financial challenges and struggles, but I loved what I was doing. About four years earlier, due to our financial challenges, I made a huge career change, working full time in the insurance industry, yet I was always doing many things for the church. Our spending habits had been poor, and for the third time, we were staring bankruptcy in the face. I personally don't believe in filing for bankruptcy, and when God said, "I will supply all your needs," I believed Him.

In my new career, I doubled and then tripled my income, yet our financial principles were completely unguided. I was desperate to learn what I had obviously not learned before, and I prayed repeatedly to God. Lo and behold, my pastor and friend at the time approached me and asked me to teach some type of financial stewardship-, budget-, money-type workshop. It was 1993, and I hadn't heard of any at the time, although there are plenty of them now.

By chance, I called this guy in Atlanta who wrote the course. I didn't really know who he was, but he was quite eager to talk to me on three Tuesday nights for an hour each about this ten-week study course that he had put together. That was Larry Burkett, and it was the grassroots of the Crown Financial Ministry.

As Larry and I had our conversations on those Tuesday nights, I saw the pieces of the puzzle coming together like never before, how every principle and every practice and all the plans were supported by scripture in the word of God. I learned that *God owns everything*—not just all my money but all my time and my talents. I learned principles about how to be successful with much or little and that He was not just my Savior and Lord but my God. I learned that if I practiced these biblical principles of stewardship, I would not only be successful but also content and happy.

We did the cash-envelope system, and they were found in my desk in my top-right drawer. My kids probably still remember those envelopes. We had each of their names on an envelope, and all their weekend activities were budgeted and put in those envelopes. I was no longer the *no* guy. The envelope was the yes or no instrument. We had sat down with the kids and shared our budget and some of these principles with them, and we all picked the amounts. So every Friday, I was at the bank getting all the small bills to put into the envelopes. I was there so often that I was even training the tellers. I revolutionized my finances forever. It was a huge personal and family victory understanding how God not only owns but also controls everything, and what's awesome is that He provides. Why *not let God have complete access to your finances?* I can promise you from personal experience that you will have greater fullness with His amazing grace and provision in your life.

The story, the moment, the appointment, the time in my life when I *knew* God was talking to me about my next growth step.

THE TRUTH LEARNED—SUCCESS

Though *success* is only mentioned once in the Bible, in Joshua 1:8, I want to use a thesaurus to illustrate the full meaning of my truth learned. I'm not just talking about financial success, which certainly can and did happen. I learned and experienced "success" in so many areas. Here are some close synonyms:

fortunate outcome, prosperous, accomplishment, victory, triumph, conquest, pre-vail, and *winning.*

Now those are some nice attributes to add to your life, don't you think?

The rest of this section was provided by my new friend, Larry Burkett. This is just some of the material he shared with me on those Tuesday evenings. Thank you, Larry, for everything. Time after time I can count the blessings of these transforming principles. Thank you, God, for the abundant riches we have in Christ Jesus. How I desire and strive to be a faithful steward for you. Amen.

AN ELEVEN-WEEK STUDY COURSE

HOW TO MANAGE YOUR MONEY BY THE CHRISTIAN FINANCIAL CONCEPT SERIES BY LARRY BURKETT
(I am only taking a few of the verses and main thoughts from each lesson summary.)

SESSION I: WHAT IS WEALTH?
Matthew 6:19–20 works with spiritual rewards in mind. The prerequisite in God's plan for wealth is "trust" in God. The Christian's wealth—those with wealth must still trust God and not be proud (1 Tim. 6:17, Ps. 17:15, Prov. 11:4). Wealth is more than just money; it is all that God gives us on this earth. Realizing this is *real* success!

SESSION II: GOD'S WILL IN FINANCES

A steward is one who "manages" but does not own (Matt. 25:14–30).

The evidence of stewardship is trust and faith in God (Luke 12:25–34)

There are eight ways God uses finances:

- Trust
- Ability to supply
- Trustworthiness
- Love
- Power
- Unification
- Direction
- Witness

Note: God can direct by supplying or withholding money. Most Christians will accept His supplying, and then borrow when He withholds.

SESSION III: THE PERILS OF MONEY

- Servitude of money (Prov. 30:7, 8, 9)
- Bondage through debt (Prov. 22:7)
- Indulgence (Luke 12:15)
- Avoiding debt (Ps. 37:21; Luke 16:12)

Conditions of servitude are "overdue bills, worry about investments, get-rich quick attitude, laziness, deceitfulness, greediness and covetousness."

Note: Stop the use of credit and many indulgences will also stop. Financial superiority is a substitute form of conceit and self-esteem. God never promised that all blessings would be material. A Christian must learn to accept, rather than dictate God's will.

SESSION IV: RELEASE FROM SERVITUDE
Larry provides ten steps to freedom

1. Transfer ownership to God (Prov. 8:18)
2. Get out of debt (Prov. 16:9)

3. Accept God's direction (Matt. 6:31)
4. Refuse quick decisions (Prov. 21:5)
5. Excel in your work (1 Pet. 4:11)
6. Confession—restitution (Luke 19:8)
7. Contentment (Eph. 5:5)
8. Provide for family needs (James 4:3 and Matt 5:42)
9. Balance commitment (Prov. 23:4–5)
10. Sacrifice desires (Eccl. 2:10, 11 and Prov. 10:22)

Note: There must be a balance between needs, wants, and desires. If we sacrifice some desires, God says that he will bless us with riches and peace.

SESSION V: FINANCIAL PLANNING PART I

This session is about setting short-range goals (Prov. 4:3–4, James 1:2–3, Prov. 20:5)

- Establish written plans and goals (Prov. 16:3)
- Commit God's portion first (Prov. 3:9–10)
- Reduce or eliminate the use of credit (Prov. 27:12)
- Seek God's plan for living within the budget (2 Chron. 16:9)
- Set your own goals (Ps. 17:15)

Note: "Credit is a subtle way to buffer God out of our decisions. Credit never avoids a decision. It only delays it and probably makes it worse."

SESSION VI: FINANCIAL PLANNING, PART II

This session is about setting long-range plans/goals.

- Why is planning and follow-up necessary? (Prov. 27:23–24)
- To know your present condition and develop God's
- Establish maximum financial goals rather than the minimum (1 Tim. 6:18–19, Luke 18:8–18).
- Establish a long-range family plan (1 Cor. 3:13, Prov. 12:22).

Note: "It is important to limit spending by establishing maximum spending goals. Otherwise there will be no surplus to invest and share in God's work."

SESSION VII: MOTIVES FOR ACCUMULATING WEALTH

- Because others advise them to save (Prov. 15:22)
- Because of envy of others (Pss. 73:2, 3; Luke 12:15)
- Because of the game of making money (Prov. 17:12)
- They accumulate for self-esteem (1 Tim. 6:17)
- They accumulate for the love of money (1 Tim. 6:10)
- They accumulate for "protection" (Pss. 50:14–15)
- They accumulate to supply a spiritual gift (2 Cor. 19:6)

Note: The Lord admonished all those who followed Him never to allow their egos to be elevated by possessions.

SESSION VIII: HOW MUCH IS ENOUGH?

This session covers four very important questions:

- How much is my current provision? (Prov. 24:30–34)
- How much for investments? (Act 4:32–35, motives)
- How much for retirement? (Eccles. 5:19–20, balance)
- How much for inheritance? (Eccles. 6:13, Prov.13:22, not indulgence)

Note: "As with almost everything else, we have developed an imbalance about retirement. It is clear that little attention is given to God's plan."

SESSION IX: SHARING BY GOD'S PLAN

- Abraham is God's first example of giving, representing God's *ownership*, not the law (Gen. 14:18–20).
- The law was God's second plan of giving, representing *obedience* (Mal. 3:8–11).

- The church has enhanced this process through the "grace of giving," representing *gratitude* (2 Cor., chapters 8 and 9).

For two whole chapters, the principle of "giving out of our abundance," "giving liberally" of themselves "out of grace" "to prove their sincerity and some gave out of their poverty" Then, in chapter 9, the *principle of sowing and reaping* is shared. "God loves a cheerful giver," given out of "bountifulness" and "thanksgiving" and giving "liberally." Why?

"Thanks be unto God for His unspeakable gift." (verse 9:15)

Note: The emphasis behind the tithe should be as a testimony of God's ownership of all that we have. The lack of giving in a Christian life is an outward sign of a lack of trust in God.

SESSION X: WHO DESERVES HELP?

- Don't help everyone (2 Thess. 3:10, 11, 14, 15; Prov. 22:9, 28:22)
- Share with your family (1 Tim 5:8 and 16; Matt. 15:5, 6)
- Share with the body (1 John 3:17–18; James 2:15,16; Matt. 24:45, 46)
- Share with the shepherds (2 Cor. 9:9–11, 14; 3 John 5, 6)
- Share with the unsaved (Matt. 5:42 and 10:42)

Note: To be a good steward included giving as well as spending. In short, it means, "don't help those who won't help themselves. Help those who can't help themselves."

SESSION XI: FINANCIAL DECISIONS

- Acknowledge His ownership—*daily* (Prov. 3:4–6, Luke 9:23)
- Accept God's answers and *direction* (Matt. 7:11, Phil. 4:6, 1 Thess. 5:18)
- Establish the minimum testimony of God's ownership (Luke 6:38)

Note: Financial breathing merely means exhaling bad financial habits and inhaling (appropriately) God's financial habit.

This is where we know in ourselves and can show to God that He is my God, who I completely trust, follow, and give to Him regularly—and no faking it now. It's the real deal!

THE TEXT EMPHASIZED
KEY PASSAGES: 2 CORINTHIANS, CHAPTERS 8 AND 9 AND LUKE, CHAPTER 16

Such huge stories are in Luke 16: the rich man and Lazarus the unjust steward; there is even "worldly wisdom and spiritual dullness in the business world," especially the main passage verses 10–13, The Stewardship of Life.

I just want to share a couple of thoughts on this passage. The *key word,* "faithful"…just being reliable and trusted, at least in the small stuff…unnoticed, unimportant. The principle of how you do the big stuff is how you do the little stuff. *Wowzer.* Counterculture there.

Verse 11 is a *key verse*; it is also a *primary thought* and a *pendulum of life.* It is also something that God can't do for you. You and only you must pass this test.

Note: it is a real test. I'm going to say it like I hear it so that everyone gets the idea. If you don't handle money correctly because it is material, how do you possibly think I would give you much more important things to have that are spiritual? You have got to be kidding me. *In other words, many Christians are not getting spiritually blessed and are unable to use these spiritual gifts because God sees how poorly they are stewards over worldly things like money and materialism.* Think about that, will you? And again. You better believe money *is* important because how you use it will determine how God will use you according to Luke 16:11–13.

Please read 2 Corinthians 8 and 9. I just don't understand why these two chapters are almost completely left out of conversation, teaching, and preaching when it comes to biblical financial attitudes. They are so clear and refreshing. The attitude of giving found in these two chapters is hardly ever taught in the churches of America. These passages talk beyond the concept of "having to give your tithe" and share the wonderful idea of the "grace of giving" and doing it cheerfully and generously. A completely different motive for giving, don't you think? Let's look at some of the highlights.

CHAPTER 8

"That in a great trial of affliction the abundance of their joy and their deep poverty abounded in the riches of their liberality" (verse 2. Wait, are you kidding me? Do you see and hear everything there that I do? That's nothing like what we think).

"They were freely willing" (verse 3b). Wow. And we give what's left over.

"They first gave themselves to the Lord, and then to us by the will of God" (verse 5b) versus our wants. Wouldn't that be wonderful?

"See that you abound in this grace also" (verse 7). That's the grace of giving, not the law.

"Testing the sincerity of your love" (verse 8c). Now that's grown-up Christianity there!

"For if there is first a willing mind…" (verse 12).

I want to end this chapter with this quote of verse 15: "As it is written [in Exod. 16:18], He who gathered much had nothing left over, and he who gathered little had no lack." Jew or Gentile, free or slave, well, it also says rich or poor…we are *all* the same in Christ.

Here are a few quotes and comments from chapter 9:

"That it may be ready as a matter of generosity and not as a grudging obligation" (verse 5b).

"But this I say: He who sows sparingly will also reap sparingly, and he who sows bountifully" (verse 6). Really, people, it's "not worth it" to be cheap with God!

"So, let each one give as he purposes in his heart, not grudgingly or of necessity; for God loves a cheerful giver" (verse 7). *Whoa!* Are we doing that? It's all about an attitude, *not* an account amount. But wait; there's more. (Doesn't that sound like a TV sales pitch? I couldn't help it. I didn't even try to stop myself.)

Look at verse 8: "And God is able [now wait, do you know God is able? To make all grace abound toward you, that you, always having all sufficiency in all things, may have an abundance for every good work." What a promise of God to us, for us. Sounds like another double dare like in Malachi 3:10. Boy it really sounds like God is wanting to bless us if we are generous—willingly.

"You are enriched in everything for all liberality, which causes thanksgiving through us to God" (verse 11). Don't we have an abundance of things to be thankful for?

"Supplies the needs of the saints, but also is abounding through many thanksgivings to God" (verse 12b). Wouldn't that be a dream come true if all people in church should have what they wanted and needed, with money left over, and they were thankful? Wow, what a dream.

Why would we ever think about doing any of this?

"Thanks be to God for His indescribable gift!" (verse 15). Can I hear an amen? Now that's what I'm talking about!

I hope you have found these passages pleasant and not burdensome. I hope you have found them refreshing and not frustrating. I hope you have found them to be freeing and not frightening. This is called being in Christ, following Him, a growth step of faith, transformation. And it is all good. Go for it.

THE TITLE OF GOD AND ITS APPLICATION "MY GOD"

Though they're not actually titles of God in themselves, there are tons of adjectives that amplify the concept. In *Vines Expository Dictionary*, the word "my" (or "mine") is a "possessive adjective of the first person, often used as a possessive pronoun with great emphasis." What that means is that despite tithing for over seventeen years and all the other wonderful growth steps, transformation, and divine moments, it wasn't until *I* gave God all my money and possessions and time and talents that I completely saw Him as *my* own personal God. Of course, I thought or knew Him to be God, like God of the universe or God Almighty or the everlasting God (and, by the way, I love those as well), *but now He is much closer*. He is *my God*. I now know without any shadow of a doubt that He really is watching out for me all the time, every time.

That way I trust Him as the owner of all that I have and believe *He* is the controller of all that I have. I must believe that He is the provider of all that I will have. Thus the "Praise God from whom *all blessings flow*. How did I get here? It's all God! His amazing graces, His own shareable riches, and that *He* cares for me (us). Though it's perhaps incomprehensible, I try to seek His unsearchable riches on a regular basis because I want to know *my God* more and more, better and better. Have you heard "He Walks with Me and He Talks with Me and He Tells Me I Am His Own"? What a great old song. So, do you see that I believe that He's *my God*?

As I understood the application of the intimate relationship that God wanted to have with me, I was overwhelmed with his intent to provide for me with superabundance. Just read Joel 2:24, Mal. 3:10, Matt. 14:20, and Luke 6:38. I love to physically illustrate that one because I got to see it happen one day on a mission trip overseas. There are also concepts of divine provision and I just can't help myself if I'm giving too many verses in this book that might scare some of you.

I believe every Christian should *memorize* the following outline:

There are six "abundants," or wants that God has already provided:

ABUNDANT JOYS

"They are abundantly satisfied with the fullness of Your house, And You give them drink from the river of Your pleasures" (Ps. 36:8).

ABUNDANT LIFE

"The thief does not come except to steal, and to kill, and to destroy. I have come that they may have life, and that they may have it more abundantly" (John 10:10)

ABUNDANT GRACE

"And God is able to make all grace abound toward you, that you, always having all sufficiency in all things, may have an abundance for every good work" (2 Cor. 9:8).

ABUNDANT POWER

"Now to Him who is able to do exceedingly abundantly above all that we ask or think, according to the power that works in us" (Eph. 3:20).

ABUNDANT SUPPLIES

"And my God shall supply all your need according to His riches in glory by Christ Jesus" (Phil. 4:19).

ABUNDANT ENTRANCE

"For so an entrance will be supplied to you abundantly into the everlasting kingdom of our Lord and Savior Jesus Christ" (2 Pet. 1:11).

So I know He is God of all, but I also know He is my God. And I just told you, "My God shall supply all of your needs according to his riches in glory in Christ Jesus" (Phil. 4:19). I hope you will occasionally say during my teaching or preaching, "Yep, that's My God." Does yours do that for you? This could be a defining moment for someone.

THE THEOLOGICAL TEACHING APPLIED THE TESTING OR TRIAL OF NOT TAKING THE STEP

1. The financial-difficulty trials won't stop until you learn this. Remember I was facing bankruptcy for the third time. (Learn quicker than I did, please. It hurts.)
2. You probably won't understand the true blessings of God.
3. Your financial mind-set will most likely be that of the world's and not Christ's—entrapment and perhaps frustration.
4. You will probably be caught up in materialism.
5. You won't let go of your money and let God, therefore, not understand the "true riches in Christ Jesus."
6. You probably won't be able to experience what God really has in mind for you.

7. Sowing sparingly means you will reap sparingly. That's financial and spiritual.
8. You'll still be sitting around thinking what you want to *get* versus thinking what you want to *give*.
9. You'll have limited experience on the concept of "It's more blessed to give than to receive (get)."
10. You will let the world's philosophy of money override the biblical teaching of the grace of giving.

THE TRIBUTE SONG

"Make Me a Blessing"
Ira B. Wilson

Out in the highways and byways of life,
many are weary and sad;
are weary and sad
Carry the sunshine where darkness is rife
making the sorrowing glad.

Refrain
Make me a blessing,
Make me a blessing,
Out of my life
out of my life
May Jesus shine;
Make me a blessing, O savior

Tell the sweet story of Christ and His love;
Tell of His pow'r to forgive;
His pow'r to forgive.
Others will trust Him if only you prove
true ev'ry moment you live.

Refrain

Give as 'twas given to you in your need;
Love as the Master loved you;
The Master loved you
Be to the helpless a helper indeed;
Unto your mission be true.

Refrain

11

Walking the Walk; Talking the Talk; Living the Life!

I T WAS NOT until thirteen years *after* my salvation that I had this resolution in my life—here we go again—that Defining Moment that ended up being a Divine Appointment. I was to be steadfast in my walk. Really, at the time of the story I'm about to tell you, it really did not matter how I felt. It no longer mattered what I thought. After this day, my family and friends and business-people no longer had any impact. It was a *conviction*, a *decision*. It even felt like rebellion against the world. But I decided to follow Jesus, and that was it.

Every day, get up, and walk with Him. In chapters 4 and 5 of Ephesians, there are five different walks that Paul illustrates for us. It's a great study by itself. It doesn't just tell us what to do but also how to be. Even in John, He uses the word "walk" in his letter.

So my story goes like this. I had graduated Bible college and had been on staff bivocational or full time for probably eight or nine years. At this time, my kids were growing up and eating more food than I could afford, and I was troubled about what to do financially. It was obvious that I had to make more money. But spiritually speaking, it was a tremendous conflict because I would be leaving the ministry, and that was where my heart and passion were.

I didn't want to quit on God. I wanted to serve Him and His people all the days of my life. But the scriptures also tell us that as the head of the household, I had the responsibility of taking care of those under my roof.

So after much prayer and with tremendous agony, I transformed out of what we would call "church work" into the secular world. It was an insurance opportunity, and the hours were all days, basically nine to five, with no weekends or nights. It had the promise of making pretty good money, but it was 100 percent commission. It was an extremely stressful decision. I had to make sales every week to pay the bills on Friday. But I trusted God and His direction as I knew it and took the tremendous leap of faith. Immediately, He blessed me beyond my wildest dreams. I worked hard, but He blessed us way beyond our expectations. But even as the excitement and stress of the new opportunity continued, I felt like somewhat spiritually empty and almost guilty.

Now, I don't know if you have conversations with God, but I do, and more than occasionally. I was thanking Him for the prosperity, and, at the same time, I was expressing frustration and sadness about no longer being in the ministry. Then God began speaking in my heart, "Jim, what do your work days and weeks look like?" I reviewed my appointments, products, and people, and it was like the Holy Spirit said, "No, the spiritual activity. Have you prayed with anybody this week?"

"Of course, Lord. Yes, I have."

"Have you encouraged any of the saints?"

"Yes, Lord, of course, I have, as time permits."

"Jim, have you shared my Hope of Salvation with anyone?"

I felt like Peter after the resurrection. *Do you love me, Peter?* Had He known about that week on a business appointment when I had dropped everything and talked people through their trials, and they had accepted Christ as their personal Savior? I didn't realize it, but, of course, He did. My heavenly Father, my everlasting sustainer, knew I was still in the ministry.

It was in 1988, *before* the Kingdom Advisors, *before* Peace University and *before* Crown Ministry, now called Compass. I gained the strength to overcome the popular opinion that the only way to serve the Lord was to work in the church—the false opinion that had created that tremendous guilt in my life. But that day, we were having a conversation, God and me. I knew in my heart that my job and my company, Strategies for Successful Retirement, were my ministry. I felt so bold, so revolutionary even, so cutting edge, so on fire, and then that night, I was reading the scriptures. I mean, you know how you read the Bible and it says something that has been there all along, but you think it's brand new? It tells us in Colossians 3:17, "Whatever you do, do it unto the Lord." I had always heard it as "whatever you do in the church," but that's not what it says. It says whatever you do, that is, any kind of job, any kind of occupation, any kind of activity, you do it unto the Lord. Talk about fortifying my heart and soul and Him being the overcomer in my life. I gladly and freely walk *steadfastly* for Him. Has something like this ever happened to you?

Now comes the story, the moment, the appointment, the time in my life when I knew God was talking to me about my next growth step.

Just like many of you, I have been doing stuff for the Lord. Most of the time, we think about *doing* something for God when, in reality, we need to be focused on *being* someone for God. Like the beatitudes and "letting this mind be in you which is in Christ Jesus." One of the most amazing characters of faith is Abraham. The reason is that he lives his entire life on two promises. One: "I'll make this land yours." It was his, but, all Abraham had then was seventy-five men who were from different countries and he was fighting for that land all the time. Do you think Abraham felt that he controlled a "nation"? Probably not so much. Nevertheless, Abraham believed God's promise.

Then God said, "You are going to be the father of many nations." Abraham didn't have even a single child until he was a senior citizen. And of course, he and Sarah did it their way, not God's way. It was years later that they finally had the child God had promised.

We can't possibly count the days and the weeks and the months. We do have a good idea of the many of years that Abraham got up and said, "Yep, this is the land God gave me. Hey, Sarah, you and I are going to be the parents of many nations," and they had absolutely nothing to show for it. What an unbelievable walk of faith and a beautiful picture of steadfastness. As it says in 1 Corinthians 15:58: "Therefore, my beloved brethren, be steadfast, immovable, always abounding in the work of the Lord, knowing that your labor is not in vain in the Lord." And I don't know how many times you and I have felt obedient to the "call" and didn't have the slightest evidence of it being fulfilled, but I'm sure it's been frequent.

THE TRUTH LEARNED

Sometimes it's so obvious that we don't see it. Yes, we still see church leaders as being more responsible (and in some ways, they are) in doing the Christian walk than the regular Christians. That concept is simply an escape clause for uncommitted followers of Christ to have an excuse to do whatever they want when the scriptures clearly say, "And whatever you do in word or deed, do all in the name of the Lord Jesus, giving thanks to God the Father through Him" (Col. 3:17).

Anyhow, we have already had this conversation, haven't we? My clear point is that we all have a responsibility to grow and grow up in Christ, to be surrendered, separated, Spirit-filled servants, and stewards for Christ. After we have taken those steps, then we need to simply be steadfast. But don't think that's the easy part. That doesn't happen until we get to heaven. (Has anybody noticed this is not heaven?) So I need, you need, we all need strength and a lot of it. Lucky for us, we can have all the strength we want or need. Amen. But it's not our strength; it is His strength that's unlimited, all power-ful, and always—yes, always—available.

The Greek word for strength is "*dunamis.*" It is also used for power, and if you say it out loud, you can imagine the word dynamite. "Dunamis" is our root word. We are talking about that kind of strength. At this point, we need to know that we have been made strong in Christ. There are a couple of words that should be abolished from our vocabulary. OK, here are the words we need to no longer have in our lives: I can't. Why not? Because we have the available strength.

We have a power that we know not.

We have access to strength that we have not yet tapped into.

We are all underachieving in God's work and His will.

The Bible stated that you have been strengthened to be steadfast. There are four different resources to get our power or strength:

First, we get this power, this strength from God Almighty. "Fear not, for I am with you; Be not dismayed, for I am your God. I will strengthen you, Yes, I will help you, I will uphold you with My righteous right hand" (Isa. 41:10).

I have so much to share here, but I really just want you to reread it three more times, pray awhile, then read it two more times, and then just claim it. Believe it. Don't let the world, the devil, or anyone else for that matter take it from you. I've got this, man! Praise the Lord! Side track...I'm looking at my notes over in Isa. 40:31, the eagle's wings. I've written what someone was preaching. Cool notes to have. The eagle had soaring power, surging power, and sticking power. Be eagles, my brothers and sisters.

Second, we get this power, this strength, from Jesus Christ. "But the Lord stood with me and strengthened me," and again in verse 18, "And the Lord will deliver me from every evil work and preserve me for His heavenly kingdom. To Him be glory forever and ever. Amen!" (2 Tim. 4:17a, 18)

Paul got deserted by everyone—his friends and fellow laborers—yet Jesus stood with him. So, my friend, you well may feel like everybody has left you (I know that feeling), yet Jesus will not only never leave you, He will also stand by you. I've been disappointed by the world; my family has scorned me for sure. I've had church people/believers do unbelievable things to me or about me. And I have also had pastors betray me (see the previous story), yet Jesus has always stood with me. I know He will be there for you too. You've got to believe this to be true all the way to heaven. Can I hear a "glory"?

Third, we get our strength or power from the Holy Spirit (Eph. 3:16). I just love this passage. It's a prayer of Paul's to the saints, and right smack dab in the middle of it all, we see our passage: "That he would grant you, according to the riches of his glory, to be strengthen with might by his spirit in the inner man." Why are we so afraid? Why are we so scared? Why are we so timid? Why are we so quiet? Why are we so powerless? Where do you get your strength? How powerful is your God? How much of the Bible will you choose to believe? How much?

Fourth, we get our strength and power from our brothers and sisters; Jesus tells Simon Peter, "But I have prayed for you, that your faith should not fail; and when you have returned to Me, strengthen your brethren" (Luke 22:32). We are to *help* each other, *strengthen* each other, *bear* each other's burdens, *bring back* our brethren, not kick them when they are down, but *build* them up, *encourage* them when they are down, and *enrich* them. I've seen so much damage in this area of the church. *Stop it!* It's not right. It doesn't work. It's embarrassing, and *it's not Godly*. Help each other, please. "Strengthen your brethren." Our strength is for good. It's used to build up, to bring back, and to lift each other up. It is a reflection of the strength we have received from God, the Father, Jesus Christ, and the Holy Spirit.

I want to share another concept with this strength—*confidence*. We need to have, show, and be confident in Christ. This paints a beautiful word picture of us "standing under" Him. It also stands for assurance and boldness and brings a quality of substance and persuasion. Here are a couple of quotes about it. "In the fear of the Lord there is strong confidence, And His children will have a place of refuge" (Prov. 14:26). "Being confident of this very thing, that He who has begun a good work in you will complete it until the day of Jesus Christ" (Phil. 1:6). There are over forty references to confidence in your concordance. I'd suggest looking them up. It's not arrogance. It's knowing, trusting, and being aware where we stand in Christ and the possibilities that He has for us. "Be strong in the Lord."

THE TEXT EMPHASIZED
FIRST CORINTHIANS 15:58 AND EPHESIANS, CHAPTERS 4 AND 5

I'm a people watcher. People are simply fascinating, unique, odd, different, and amazing. The simple process of walking is extremely diverse. Let me give an example. Boys and girls who are five to seven years old don't walk. They skip, jump, hop, turn cartwheels, and bounce. You name it. They do everything but walk. As a parent, this sometimes annoyed me, but as a grandparent, I find so much humor in it—hysterical fascination. This is partly because the parents are bothered too. A little advice, parents: enjoy it, and let it go. They will have plenty of time in life to just walk. Let them enjoy their "transporting" as they wish, and you just enjoy it too.

I say this because I also watch the much older couples walking through the mall. It's work. It's hard, and it hurts. They hold hands enough to support each other, so focused on every step, and aware of all that is around them and the obstacles (steps) ahead. Trying to be as safe and careful as possible, they accomplish one more trip successfully. What a different walk they have from the children. There are also many parallels in our spiritual walk.

There are so many different walks, but I'll just mention a few. The "shoppers"—they are looking everywhere, but where are they going? The "fashion walk" as if they are on a fashion-show prance. The muscular guy power walker who is all puffed up. The "person on a mission" targeting the gaps through all the others. And then there are the people who just kind of go aimlessly, taking up the aisle completely, unaware of others. The list goes on. People have pictures of their spiritual walks too. We will see that later.

FIRST CORINTHIANS 15:58

Everyone, and I do mean *everyone,* should memorize this scripture. *If* you choose this growth step, you must *memorize this one verse* and be familiar with the whole passage in verses 51–58. I'm going to quote Kenneth S. West in his new book, *The New Testament—An Expanded Translation*: "So that my brethren beloved, keep on becoming steadfast, unmovable, always abounding in the work of the Lord, knowing that your fatiguing is not unproductive of results, as this labor is done in the Lord." Now, isn't that saying something so significant, so powerful, so clear? The life message of so many key words. Break down each word and apply them where you are right now and tomorrow. It's continuous, ongoing, and productive no matter how we feel. *Keep going. What a goal.* What *encouragement.* What a *command.* What a *comfort.* What a *conquest.* What a *calling.*

OUR OTHER PASSAGE IS FOUND IN EPHESIANS, CHAPTERS 4 AND 5.

We are going to actually go through this passage in our teaching section, so let me use this part to emphasize the "walking" concept in the Bible and in these passages. To walk implies three things: purpose—starting on a goal, progress—advancing step by step, and *perseverance*—keeping on until the goal is reached.

Are you ready to walk—imitate and follow Christ in you? These two chapters will cover five different purposes/kinds of walk:

1. A worthy walk of the vocation
2. Walk as a new man (person)
3. Walk as children of love
4. Walk as children of light
5. By walking with wisdom.

They are going to expand on these concepts with an underlying continued message of:

- walking worthy in unity encourages the body of Christ in Love.
- "imitate"—copy, duplicate, impersonate, mimic, "be like."

- followers—adherent, attended devotee, disciple, successor, supporter.
- to follow—succeed, come next, comply, heed, obey, observe, adopt, copy, chase, pursue, train, ensue.

Walking stands for steady, sustained motion and evokes action

- of *the mind* in the decision to start,
- of *the heart* in the desire to continue, and
- of *the will* in the determination to arrive.

Note: it is something only we can do ourselves. That could be why so few do it or make it this far. But there is more: the Christian is to walk *in newness of life* (Rom. 6:4) after the *spirit* (8:4) in *honesty* (13:13), by *faith* (2 Cor. 5:7) in *good works* (Eph. 2:10), *in love* (5:2), *in wisdom* (Col. 4:5), in *truth* (2 John 4) after the *commandments of the Lord* (verse 6). And negatively, *not* after the flesh (Rom. 8:4), *not* after the manner of men (1 Cor. 3:3), *not* in craftiness (2 Cor. 4:2), *not* be sight (5:7), *not in the vanity of the mind* (Eph. 4:17), and *not* disorderly (2 Thess. 3:6).

Some other great passages

"Stand fast therefore in the liberty by which Christ has made us free, and do not be entangled again with a yoke of bondage" (Gal. 5:1).

"Do not be deceived, God is not mocked; for whatever a man sows, that he will also reap. For he who sows to his flesh will of the flesh reap corruption, but he who sows to the Spirit will of the Spirit reap everlasting life. And let us not grow weary while doing good, for in due season we shall reap if we do not lose heart" (Gal. 6:7, 8, 9).

"Only let your conduct be worthy of the gospel of Christ, so that whether I come and see you or am absent, I may hear of your affairs, that you stand fast in one spirit, with one mind striving together for the faith of the gospel" (Phil. 1:27).

"Resist him, steadfast in the faith, knowing that the same sufferings are experienced by your brotherhood in the world" (1 Pet. 5:9).

THE TITLE OF GOD AND ITS APPLICATION
EVERLASTING—OVERCOMER—SUSTAINER—
EVERLASTING

Really? Everlasting? We don't have *any* concept of this at all—*none*. Lifetime— well, it's just a vapor. Years—they're just seconds. Yet "our God," my God is everlasting. That's cool, awesome, powerful, so encouraging, always, and I do mean *always…amazing…*this means that no matter how we feel, and no matter how low we can get in life.

Story time! In the South, we have a phrase, "I'm so down that I'm lower than a snake's belly." Remember my days sleeping in the tree? Well one night, it was a little cool to say the least, and I was covered in a blanket. In the middle of the night, I felt this weight on my chest and stomach. Don't forget, I was up in a tree. I slowly looked, and there was this four-foot red rat snake (AKA corn snake) lying on top of me. Now, this was *real*. As I lay there thinking about all the things I could do, I realized that the snake just wanted to keep warm. I had seen it around before, and it was a quite calm snake. So there I was, in the middle of the night, twenty feet up in the tree, and my thoughts were that no one else loved me or even trusted me, but this snake did. He found comfort and trust in me. Well I liked that, so I just went back to sleep with it lying there, keeping warm. It was gone when I got up the next morning. So yes, I have been "low" before—lower than a snake's belly. I didn't know God then, but I do know Him now. And I can tell you with complete confidence, He is my *always, everlasting, eternal, present God*. And I needed that; you need that to keep up your steadfast walk to keep going.

As we look at the definition, it talks about an undefined endless time. That is beyond "time." Yeah, just go ahead and try to wrap your brain around that one.

Moreover, it is used of persons and things that are in their very nature endless, or of God (Rom. 16:26), of His power (1 Tim. 6:16), and of His glory (1 Pet. 5:10) of the Holy Spirit (Heb. 9:14), of the redemption effected by Christ (Heb. 9:12), and of the consequent salvation of men (5:9), as well as of His future rule (2 Pet. 1:11), which is elsewhere declared to be without end (Luke 1:33) of the life received by those who believe in Christ (John 3:16), concerning whom He said "they shall never perish," (2 Cor. 5:1), elsewhere said to be immortal, (1 Cor. 15:53), in which that life will be finally realized (Matt. 25:46, Tit. 1:2).

OVERCOMER

Remember we are in a battle, and it is nonstop and can intensify as you grow in Christ, and there are many battles you will win. But there are those who will struggle; the fight will be hard, and sometimes long and perhaps spiritually exhausting. We have an "overcomer God." "These things I have spoken to you, that in Me you may have peace. In the world, you will have tribulation; but be of good cheer, I have overcome the world" (John 16:33). That just makes me laugh with joy, peace, and confidence. *Overcome* is defined as conquer, the "mightiest prevail." Well that's the side I want to be on.

Here is a list of applications:

1. of God the mightiest (Rom 3:4)
2. of Christ (John 16:33, Rev. 3:21)
3. of His followers (that's us!) (Rom. 12:21; 1 John 2:13, 14, and 4:4 and the seven churches in Revelation)
4. of Faith (1 John 5:4, 5)
5. of evil (Rom. 12:21)

JAMES H. WILLIS III

The point is that we have a lot of help to take this journey, and it's the most powerful help we can get. We will win in the end. The Overcomer has *already won*. We are just passing through.

SUSTAINER

How would you like it if you knew you had support—someone to hold you up, to take the brunt of the troubles and pain, to keep you, keep you up, and keep you going? How about someone who would supply your every need? Someone could and would provide for you like no other? Well, that's what I found when I decided to continue in my walk, whether others did or did not. Whether it was easy or hard, popular or not, I choose to be continual, consistent, and convicted to continue my walk with Christ and have that "steadfast walk." And when I did that "by faith," just like all the other Defining Moments that were really Divine Appointments, God showed up in a brand-new way.

How do I keep on going? Ha well, it's not by my strength and power. I know when I'm doing that. It's exhausting, hard, depressing, and defeating. But in His power—it's endless, hopeful, powerful, and exciting! Why? Because he is my Everlasting, Overcomer, and Sustainer. See passages in Psalm 3:5, 55:22 and Isaiah 9:16 for many other applicable stories, parables, and applications.

THE THEOLOGICAL TEACHING EPHESIANS, CHAPTERS 4 AND 5 WALK WITH A WITNESS

The book of Ephesians is basically divided into three subjects. Chapters 1, 2, and 3 talk about the Christian's wealth—oh my, the riches we have in Christ Jesus. Chapters 4 and 5 identify the Christian's *walk* or lifestyle if you please. And chapter 6:10–23 obviously prepares us for *warfare*. We are just doing an overview of chapters 4 and 5. These identify five different walks.

Walking is simply" keeping on..keeping on!" It's perseverance and endurance and having confidence or purpose in your destination. I don't have any doubt in this journey. I'll get there. Therefore, it is *hope*, seeing the end in mind even if it is unseen. "Now faith is the substance of things hoped for, the evidence of things not seen" (Heb. 11:1).

Simply put, it's a step-by-step process. As I looked at people's walking styles in the malls, they are *all* very different. Similarly, your Christian walk is very individualized and unique. *Yet all our walks have these five characteristics* because they are all Christ-like in nature and character, yet unique in style. God works the same in all of us, but He likes to do it differently. Thus, this book is *my* story of my growth in Christ. What's yours? I hope and pray you are developing one even now.

1. WALK WORTHY OF THE VOCATION (EPH. 4:1–6, 12, 16)
Are you ready to walk immediately and follow Christ in you? That means you're constantly conducting yourself Christ-like. From jail, Paul is telling you right off the bat. You don't have any excuses. If I'm doing it in jail, so can you. So start now because it's a calling. It's not really an option, people. *You are here for this purpose*, and the Bible says live like Christ at your job (vocation). Wowzers. I know that's counterculture, counter government, and against everything. But it wasn't the "in thing" to do then either. But let's look at why Jesus is asking us to do it.

First let's see the attitude we are supposed to have—words like lowliness, not prideful; meekness equals equality; long-suffering equals patience. Why don't we do all this? We are to be caring about the people around others not caring about ourselves. God does that! Did you just hear that? I'm saying it again. Our walk, in order for it to be "worthy," is a walk or lifestyle that cares about those around us. We shouldn't care for ourselves, because God cares for us. It's a *life-changing principle, people.*

Second, look what it *does to the body* of Christ, the church. Tremendous, unity, power, care, purpose. It's loving and includes everybody. No cliques. Everyone, every day, always encouraging (edifying) everybody. Doesn't that sound like a dream come true? It is, and it can be because it's your calling and purpose. When we do this, it's powerful and enriching. It's lovely. When we think about our jobs right now, just think what would and could happen if we worked like Paul just described. Or in our churches, what if all our ideas and plans were what Jesus wants our church to be doing, and if we are all doing it in unity and love and preferring one another instead of ourselves.

What's your vocation, job, and ministry? Are you walking worthy of your vocation?

2. WALK AS A NEW MAN (EPH. 4:17–32)

This passage has some of the most powerful and practical principles in all the Christian's teaching. Simply put, if you don't do these simple principles, you won't do much in your Christian walk. These steps are fundamentally important for your personal success. I really want you to be successful, Christians. This is how you start. We are going to look at four P words: position, put off, put on, and put away.

Now the first is position of the old man. The "old man" is who we were before we came to Christ. The "new man" is us living in Christ. We have got to quit lying to ourselves and stop comparing ourselves to others. They don't count. The only measuring stick to our holy, righteous is God Almighty. And when we are all honest with ourselves, words like "vanity," "darkness," "separated," and "blind" refer to all our lives, our hearts, our minds, and our bodies at one time in our past life—even if you got saved as a cute church kid at six are still all true. Be honest with yourself. You know it's true. Why fake it? Our first step to a *new man* is to know our position.

Second, put off the old man. Verse 22 is so fascinating in how simple it all is. It all starts with believing God. Did He love you? Did He forgive you? Did He make you His child to live with Him forever? Of course He did. OK then, just "take off" that old man. Consider him to be dead, because he is.

There is no life in it—*none*. And stop living that way, acting that way, and sounding that way. *Just stop it*, or *just say no* to the power of the flesh, and say yes to the new man.

Third, put on the new man. You can't put on the new person until you have taken off the old person. Covering that one up won't work. It won't last. You have to come clean getting rid of that filthy old man. Throw it all away, and then put on the new person. You've got to claim the New You. It is your new position in Christ Jesus. It is the new you! You also have to want it, to covet it, to desire it, and to possess it. It is your wealth, as described in chapters 1–3. And then you need to count on it. Rely on it. It is your new power—the power of the Holy Spirit as promised. This is how you got it. And while you're putting on the new man, look at the whole armor of God as described in Ephesians 6:10–18. Now that's putting on a new look wouldn't you think?

Fourth, putting away the old man equals carnal life, the old lifestyle, that old you. Oh, he won't go completely away. But we must put him away continually, all the time. Nope, he won't stop trying to raise his ugly self back into our lives. But with Christ, Holy Spirit, and our brothers and sisters in Christ, we can *keep* putting him away—way back, way down. What God has already done for us positionally, He longs for us to live out that victory. Being like Christ, following Him…Oh, that's a Christian.

3. WALK AS CHILDREN OF LOVE (EPH. 5:1–7)
Little children just have the purest of love. They are so honest without any reservations. And as parents, we would do anything for our kids. Well God wants us to love as dear little children, not like an adult. As adults, there are so many conditions, reservations, and hesitations. Not so for little kids. I mean, we know how much God loves us, how Jesus already died for all of our sin, and how the Holy Spirit works with us all the time. God wants us to just take all that on with pure childlike faith. "Let the children come to me," Jesus said. Now again, walk with me again as little children with blind faith.

There is also a lot of "bad love" out there that tries to cover up the real love. They are distorting God's perfect plan and are out of place for the Christians. The long list is simple things that children of God should no longer be doing—you know, put off, put on, and putting away. Love like God loves you. This walk and this lifestyle is something only we can do for ourselves!

4. Walk as Children of Light (Eph. 5:8–14)

Light in the Bible is a fascinating concept. God is the Father of light. Jesus is the light of the world. The Holy Spirit enlightens men's hearts, and we are to be God's "little lights" all over the world. Oh yes, we were in darkness, but now we are in the light. Light helps plants grow. Light warms the souls of mankind. Light, in itself, can be the source of hope.

So when we are asked to "walk in light," what does that look like? It is to reveal the fruits of the spirit. There are nine of them. We are to be displaying goodness (be good to people) with righteousness as well as truthful to all. Though we are to pull away or separate from the unfruitful, we still are to correct and call out their ungodliness and reveal the bad works or deeds. The only way we are going to keep ourselves in the light and be the light is to continually worship the Light. The light of God *awakes* us and gets us spiritually awake. It also *arises* in us to be physically alert, and finally it is *alive* in us, creating that godly glow.

So are you walking as a child or as an adult with God? Really ask yourself, what is the voltage of your light?

5. By Walking with Wisdom (Eph. 5:15–21)

I saw a local church sign that read, "God is not looking for religious nuts but spiritual fruits." This is so funny and true. Just because we are Christians doesn't mean we need to be weird. Yes, we are different from the world because of our faith. But we don't have to be cold or awkward socially or intelligently. There is a process to how we receive information and grow toward wisdom. The *first step* is information or facts. We may not know or understand those facts, but they are true. Second is knowledge, having the application of the accumulated facts and putting them together. And third is wisdom, and with wisdom comes understanding. It's not just facts and information but also the creation of ideas and the understanding of how they work as well as developing thoughts. And God himself is asking us to walk with wisdom. Read Proverbs every day, one chapter for each day of the month.

We will need to find our purpose. And the only way to do that is to get God's perspective, fit into His timing, and then you will be able to follow God's will. Next in our passage, we need to continually be aware of our power source—it's God. We want our new man in power every day. Not the old man. We will also keep our hearts worshipping Him in every way, with powerful self-talk and a sweet-smelling sacrifice of praise.

By the way, has anybody noticed that we are having a big church divide going on over music? Anybody? How about everybody? Let me share this one of many biblical concepts versus your personal preferences. Ephesians 5:19 says, psalms, hymns, spiritual songs (praises). Notice something—God likes all three. Not one or the other, but *all three*—at the same time, same place. All *three*, people. But none is worth singing unless you are singing to God with your whole heart. I'm just sayin' what the book is sayin'. That's all I've got to say about that.

So we are to walk in wisdom. To follow Christ, take heed of His ways, adapt, copy, and imitate Christ all the way. How you doing?

THE TESTING OR TRIALS OF NOT TAKING THE STEP

1. It's the whole point of being a Christian or a Christ follower, or you will be out of touch all the way through your life.
2. You will be outwardly disobedient to God's desire for you.

3. You will not likely have a spiritual foundation, so you will likely be pushed around emotionally and bounced around with all kinds of false doctrine.
4. You will lack confidence and power in your life.
5. You will not be an attractive "witness" for the Gospel's sake.
6. You will miss out on God's overcoming power in your obstacles of life.
7. You will likely not understand God's everlasting purpose and sustaining gifts in your life.

These are all so sad. Why not have that Defining Moment with God today and make it a Divine Appointment?

THE TRIBUTE SONG

"I Want to Be Like Jesus"
Text: Thomas O. Chisholm
Music: David Livingstone Ives

I have one deep supreme desire,
That I may be like Jesus.
To this I fervently aspire,
That I may be like Jesus.
I want my heart his throne to be,
So that a watching world may see
His likeness shining forth in me.
I want to be like Jesus.
He spent His life in doing good;
I want to be like Jesus.
In lowly paths of service trod;
I want to be like Jesus.
He sympathized with hearts distressed;
He spoke the words that cheered and blessed;
He welcome sinners to His breast.
I want to be like Jesus.
A holy harmless life He led;
I want to be like Jesus.
The Father's will, His drink and bread;
I want to be like Jesus.
And when at last He comes to die,
"Forgive them, Father" hear Him cry
For those who taunt and crucify.
I want to be like Jesus.
Oh, perfect life of Christ, my Lord!
I want to be like Jesus.
My recompense and my reward,

That I may be like Jesus.
His Spirit fill my hungr'ing soul,
His power all my life control;
My deepest pray'r, my highest goal,
That I may be like Jesus.

12

WHERE IS "HERE" ANYWAY?

FINAL THOUGHTS—A GRATEFUL perspective

Jim, do you know where that tree is? It's a question I get asked all the time. Shortly after living in it, I did visit it occasionally. But that *entire area*—miles and miles of woods—has been completely developed. So, no, I have no idea now. But in my own mind, I hope it's the centerpiece of the neighborhood park, where many kids have been able to climb up it and play under it, and certainly, I hope it has provided shade for many family picnics and childhood games.

And really "the tree" was not a happy place. Unique, yes, but happy—well, no. Those were extremely difficult times. The tree was all I had—well, that and a large appliance box on the ground full of all my possessions. It was the peak of the rawest, saddest, and the most desperate time in my life. I had nothing. I had nobody. And I felt that way too—a nothing, a nobody.

Believe me, it's all quite true. I was unloved, unwanted, and uncared for in every way. Way deep down I heard these voices, these annoying thoughts in my head or heart, I didn't really know which. But I would just scream at the top of my lungs at the stars in the sky, because everything inside of my heart and soul was just crying out, "*I don't want to be a nobody! I want to be a somebody!*" Now does this mean I am somebody now? Well, I can answer that with "my story". It's a great lesson that I share whenever I'm doing a motivational, self-esteem talk to kids and adults. Have you ever had this dream or thought of being somebody, yet you feel like a big nobody? I can tell you that anyone can be transformed into a somebody because God loves everybody. And all nobodies can grow into a somebody. By-the-way, to God, there are not any nobodies.

I know I may not be a somebody to you. But nevertheless, I am a somebody, first of all, to me. I personally know I've grown, changed, and yet stayed me. It's *all me, all the time*, and today (and for years) I've come to love me, even as I am. I'm happy and for the most part and living way beyond the dreams I had back when survival was my priority. We all measure success differently—here's how I look at it.

The first one I'll mention is my *self-esteem*. It's good! But hey, it's not all due to me. Second, my *business/career* has changed my life since 1988. I've had the opportunity to travel the world and stay in five-star resorts—beautiful amazing places. I've traveled to most of the American states. What a great country we have! Third, my ministry. Of course, I want to do more. Of course, I wish I could have done more. But you know what? Where I came from, I'm blessed to have done any.

For example, none of my family and certainly not my old high-school mates would ever dream that I would go to college and pass while I worked thirty-six hours a week. I did well actually. I was the first one in my family to go to college, and I got a Bachelor of Science degree in theology of all things. Go figure. I went on to be associate pastor in three churches and a faithful, impacting member after that. When my kids grew up and moved out of the house (I'll get to them in a minute), I was able to start fulfilling a dream of taking short-term international mission trips. I must admit that I'm addicted to them. We—Candi, my wife, and I (I'll get to her in a minute too)—have been on dozens of mission trips around the world. Now, those accommodations are *not* five stars. They are something like one or two stars. Or they could be a "multitude of stars" because sometimes we sleep underneath the sky full of stars in a hammock. Amazing, memories of "the tree." The mission trips remind me all the time how far I've come and how much I have.

But let me go to my favorite part, the best changes. The evidence of "how on earth I got here...from there"? Remember my "there" was quite difficult and violent, with lots of conflict; it was actually quite horrible. But now my relationship with my family has mostly grown wonderfully. My dad and my younger sister accepted Christ into their lives and have done well growing in Him. My dad passed in 1994, knowing that he was safe and secure in Christ. My little brother, well, he is a story all by himself. We enjoy each other immensely.

Wait for it; here it comes. It's been a long journey for sure, but my older sister and I are getting along great these days. We really enjoy each other! Wow, miracles happen.

As you have seen, for a lifetime my relationship with my mom had been very difficult in every way. Yet – another answer to prayer - in recent months, for the first time we have a positive relationship. Some of our conversations have even included spirituality. We continue to pray for her.

Now between Candi and me, we have five kids. I raised three: Joshua, Jason, and Joslynn. No valedictorians, but two class clowns. Too funny, right? They all excelled in sports, a variety of them nonstop and now they have given us *grandkids.* Nobody told me about grandkids and being a grandpa. The grandkids call me Grampy Jim. This stuff is *fun.* Lots of lovin', playing, and teasing, and they like me. This is a cool thing. They are so much fun. I get to teach them all kinds of stuff. I'm not telling what, though—their parents might read the book. I am so proud of my kids. Young adults, excuse me—or maybe they're just adults now. They and their spouses are wonderful, successful active people in their communities.

And then there are Candi's two daughters, Janet and Pam. They are amazing, talented ladies who are such giving people. They are a little too smart for me—teachers, college master's degrees, and they are so talented. And they love me too. Go figure. The three grandkids they gave us came first and have been a blast. They are way too much fun, riding roller coasters, fishing, riding horses, sleepovers where we build forts, and on and on. We are ready for more. Pam's husband, Bryan, a police officer on the SWAT team, is like a son to me. I love when he calls to share his latest adventure with me. The family all fits together with who they are. (Oh, a special footnote: Pam has been doing most/all of the first-draft typing. That means she had to read my handwriting for the entire book. *Wowzers.* "Thank you" just isn't enough.) I'm blessed beyond measure, but one way to measure is our ten grandkids/playmates—oh, fun!

Next is my wife, Candi. Other than the obvious involvement of the sovereignty of God in both our lives, I have absolutely no idea how I could score this big. She is my best friend in everything. She even worked with me full time for fourteen years. We do just about everything together. Remember all those years of being unloved? Living with Candi has made up for it all. Living with her lets me wake up with dreams in my heart and go to sleep at night filled with thankfulness. She is my "sweet thing"—get it? Yes, I am addicted to a few things, and the main one is Candi! Get it again? OK. OK. I'll stop. There are a lot more, but remember that I'm a guy, and guys don't get all mushy. One more thing about my Candi: she is my main "*here!*" To me, she is a gift straight from God. She is the most lovable, and loving person I have ever known. Thank you, Candace Jean, for all that you and I are. I have no idea where I'd be without you.

And most importantly is Jesus. He is the why, the who, the how, the what, and the where of how I got *here.* That night in the movie theater was the first time I heard that anybody loved me, and it was God! That made an impact all right. It changed me, changed my life, changed my plans and desires, changed everything…thus the real reason for this book.

He—Jesus Christ—really wanted to have a personal relationship with me. He had this huge plan, and though I didn't know about it at the time, He wanted me to be a part of it. Can you believe that? I did and still do, *forty years later.* In this journey I have gone through, God alone has filled the voids in my life, and as you know, there were plenty. Jesus has healed so many of the wounds in my life: emotional, physical, relationship-wise, and spiritually. He made me whole. Praise God! That's my story, and I'm sticking to it.

WRAP UP AND ENCOURAGEMENT

I want to end the book with a summary and challenge. Our last growth step was being steadfast, unmovable, and always abounding in the work of the Lord. Isn't that just so clear and easy to understand? Then why not just obey and do it?

I'd like to share a couple of very important life points here. *If you choose to be obedient to the voice and calling of God Almighty and clearly take the steps of transformation, you will realize you are not done.* We are never done until we are gone. Period. The three enemies are still here, and they will not leave us alone. In many ways, the battles get bigger. The test will continue, and our faith will need to grow more. We are never done shining the light, living the message, and loving the lost. And those three enemies hate it. Satan and all his demons will still come after us in all the sly ways he has used since the Garden of Eden. The world is still corrupt—even more so now, and our Christian faith is all countercultural, against the grain of this world, and we will again need to stay strong and determined not to be like the world.

And then there is that dirtiest enemy of all—the deceptions, the lies, the guilt, the doubts. All of them and more come from within ourselves. That fallen nature just won't shut up no matter how many times we kill it. But there is coming a day—it will be a glorious day that the "old man" will be gone and not just spiritually speaking, but practically speaking. Realize it will be done once and for all, whether it is at death (it dies, praise God), and we go to heaven with our new heavenly bodies or at the rapture when we all get transported at once when we meet Jesus in the air. "Oh, what a glorious day that will be when Jesus I shall see, when He takes my hand and leads me through the promised land, what a day, glorious day that will be." Praise God!

But until that day, we will have trials and troubles and will be tested because we are still in the battle of life and death for the souls of men and women all around us. I'm asking you to get in the game. The Church needs Christians growing in Christ, desperately not staying the same, doing a few religious things and doing some selfish worldly things. "Choose you this day whom you will serve." Come on, the church *needs you* badly! Our communities need us. They don't think so, but they do. Who are they going to call in times of trouble? You guessed it—us. And we have got to be ready to give an answer of hope, love, peace, and joy.

And last, God wants you. I still get a lump in my throat, I still get chills in my body, and I still don't understand why really, but this one thing I do know...God Almighty loves me more than I can understand, and He really does want to have an intimate, loving, powerful relationship with me. And he won't quit. He won't stop trying. And every time I finally listened to Him and took that amazing, ridiculous growth step of faith, He has always—I mean *always*—wowed me and amazed me. Why didn't I do this before? I know better. I still want to do better.

So how about you? Do you want to grow up in Christ? Do you want to have a closer relationship with God Almighty, Savior, Lord, the Holy One? I have shown you how. That's the point of the whole book. The why, and the what, most of you know. But this is all about the how. Those Defining Moments in life...don't let them pass on by. Grab them by faith, and respond obediently to God, and make them Divine Appointments. Make it your story, your victory, your overcoming moment, your steps in Christ Jesus, and your transformation to be more like Him so that your faith, joy, and hope will be stronger in you. Then God Himself will be revealed in your life in a fuller way and you too will be telling your stories about how God worked in your life. Now that's what I'm writing about, because that's what the Bible has already written. Paul says come and "follow me as I follow Christ." So, do it. Come on. I can promise you that it will change your life, forever.

Epilogue

One Last Story—I'm Back in a Tree!

I T WAS THE last day of our 2017 International Mission Trip to the Dominican Republic. We'd had a great week. We had done Vacation Bible School with hundreds of kids; we had shared Jesus through street evangelism, and we had worked with and fed the homeless people who lived at the city dump. (Homeless…Whoa, I had impactful flashbacks.)

I was given the chance to preach at an English-speaking church, and I was so excited. The morning was hectic. Everybody was busy, excited, and packing, and there was just a lot going on. We had to be on time, or we'd miss our plane that was leaving right after church. The worship leader was leaving early with all the equipment, and he asked me if I would like to go with him, so I'd have time to pray before preaching. I jumped at the opportunity.

I had no idea where the church service was going to be—and, well, surprise! We stopped at a fantastic resort. I carried supplies through the complex and approached a beautiful pavilion built in Tiki-hut style right on the beach with waves crashing over the rocks fifty feet behind the pulpit. There was gorgeous white sand and lounge chairs. As I sat in one of the lounge chairs, I soaked in the moment. It took me back to the old days when I often had nowhere to sleep, and I'd just find a quiet spot on the beach. The waves rhythmically slapping the shoreline seemed to wash away all my frustrations.

It quickly got warm sitting in the chair on the beach. I could tell there was a breeze up in the trees, but I wasn't able to feel it. I began looking around for a place where I could go to feel the breeze and see and hear the water, and then *wham, there it was, a* tree. A leaning sea grape tree, right on the beach. Even though I was all cleaned up to preach, I could easily get up in that tree, right? Absolutely! And so up I went.

I started to review my sermon, but my mind and all my senses were becoming overwhelmed. The memories just started flooding my heart, soul, and spirit. I had come full circle.

I was in a tree, but this time it wasn't for survival; it was simply for joy. This time when I was on the beach, I was not lonely; I was loved and appreciated. And this time, as I contemplated my life, I wasn't in a horrible, empty place, needy, and without hope; I was full—full of life and full of love. I had more than I ever dreamed possible when I was living in that tree, and I was getting ready to share the message of God's love, peace, joy, and hope that we can all have.

Yes, I was having another Holy Spirit–inspired moment. I was full of wonder and gratefulness.

I had planned my message several weeks before, but can you guess what it happened to be on? *"Anybody can be a somebody."* It was out of the passage found in Ephesians 2:1–10. I was personally a little overwhelmed too. Thank you, Jesus!

The scriptures give a beautiful comparison of the "old man" and the "new workman" in Christ Jesus. To me, an important phrase is found in verse 4: "But God." None of this would have happened if God hadn't intervened in my life. God saved me physically, mentally, emotionally, and spiritually, just like the passage says. "But God."

Sitting in the tree on that beach in the Dominican Republic, I was so lost in the moment with God and my memories that I was unaware that everyone had arrived for church. As I preached the message, it was so personal that I became very passionate; it was God's message tied to my story. It was a beautiful moment.

Don't ever try to tell me God doesn't care about us. I am living proof that He does. I was on a path to destruction. *"But God."* Hmmm, that may be a good title for my next book.

Blessings to you all. I will leave you with my life verse: "Now to Him who is able to keep you from falling, and to present you faultless before the presence of His glory with exceeding joy." (Jude 24).

Happy in Him,
Jim

Picture by Wiley Edward Davis

I would love to hear back from you about your stories, your growth steps or transformation, and your Defining Moments & Divine Appointments. Please write me at: JimWillisbooks@gmail.com. And may you grow in the grace and knowledge of the Lord Jesus Christ.

Jim would love to share his story, and his love and passion for Christ, at your church, men's group, or youth department. You can contact him at: JimWillisBooks@gmail.com.